The Dad's Faith Guide

A 52-Week Devotional for Christian Dads

© Tiffany Barker

A GIFT FOR

____

FROM

____

DATE

____

Thank you message

Thank you for choosing this devotional and allowing it to be a part of your fatherhood journey. As I wrote each page, I thought about the dedication, challenges, and love you pour into your family every day. It's truly an honor to walk with you over the course of these 52 weeks, and I pray that each devotion offers you encouragement, wisdom, and strength.

You carry a great responsibility, and in that, you reflect the heart of our Heavenly Father. My hope is that these reflections will remind you of the strength and grace God provides, especially during those tough moments when you feel overwhelmed. On the brighter days, may these words celebrate the joy of fatherhood and the powerful impact you have on your children and family.

From my heart to yours, thank you for allowing me to be a small part of your walk with God. May He continue to guide and uplift you as you lead your family with faith, love, and purpose.

Table of contents

Introduction

Overview of the Devotional's Purpose

Fatherhood is a blessing, but it also comes with challenges that can feel overwhelming. Every day, dads face the demands of providing for their families, raising their children in a world filled with distractions, and striving to grow spiritually despite the busyness of life. Many fathers want to be godly men who lead their families in faith, but the pressures of work, home, and personal commitments often pull them in different directions. Balancing all these responsibilities can leave fathers feeling worn out and unsure of how to grow in their spiritual walk while meeting the demands of everyday life.

This devotional is designed to address the realities that Christian fathers face. It acknowledges that fatherhood is both joyful and demanding and that spiritual growth can seem impossible when time and energy are limited. This book, The Dad's Faith Guide: A 52-Week Devotional for Christian Dads, serves as a practical, encouraging resource to help fathers navigate the complexities of their roles with faith as their foundation. It is meant to be a guide for fathers seeking to integrate their spiritual life with their responsibilities as husbands, providers, and leaders of their families.

Each week, this devotional will address a specific struggle that fathers face. From feeling overwhelmed by the weight of responsibility to managing time between faith and family, this devotional will provide biblical wisdom, personal reflections, practical steps, and prayers to encourage dads in their journey. These weekly readings will help fathers to stay grounded in their faith, even when life gets busy. The aim is to strengthen your relationship with God, while equipping you with the spiritual tools to lead your family with love, grace, and wisdom.

Unlike devotionals that require lengthy readings or theological depth, this book is crafted for busy dads who need quick but meaningful insights. Each week's reflection is designed to be read in about 15 minutes, with action steps that can easily fit into your daily routine. Whether you're starting your morning with this devotional, reading during a lunch break, or winding down in the evening, these weekly messages will help you realign your focus on Christ and lean on God's strength.

This devotional is not about achieving perfection. As fathers, we often fall short. But by turning to God, we are reminded that He doesn't expect perfection from us. He asks for faithfulness. Through this devotional, you will be encouraged to trust in God's grace, to rely on His wisdom, and to find peace in knowing that you are not walking this path of fatherhood alone.

You are not just a father by chance—you are a father by God's design. He has placed you in this role for a purpose, and He will equip you with everything you need to succeed. You will find strength in His Word, guidance through prayer, and comfort in knowing that you can rely on God in every season of fatherhood. This devotional is here to walk alongside you on that journey.

Let's begin this journey of faith together, one week at a time.

Words of Encouragement for Fathers

Balancing Spiritual Growth, Family Leadership, and Daily Challenges

As a father, it's easy to feel stretched too thin. The responsibilities of family life often leave little time or energy for your personal spiritual growth. Whether you're working attending to your children's needs, or supporting your spouse, it can feel like there's always more to do and never enough hours in the day. In these moments, it's easy to place your own spiritual needs on the back burner, assuming you'll get to them eventually. However, maintaining your spiritual connection with God is not a luxury, but a necessity that will sustain you through the challenges of fatherhood.

God calls you to be the spiritual leader of your home, but He doesn't expect you to do it alone. The demands of family life may be great, but God's grace is greater. He knows the pressures you face, and He promises to provide strength and wisdom to help you meet those challenges. One of the greatest gifts you can give to your family is the example of a father who walks closely with God. When your spiritual life is in alignment with God's will, everything else in your life begins to fall into place.

The key to balancing spiritual growth with the responsibilities of fatherhood is to remember that your strength comes from God. The more you rely on His strength, the less burdened you'll feel by the pressures of life. When you start your day in prayer or spend time meditating on Scripture, you invite God into every aspect of your life. This daily connection with God doesn't need to be long or complicated. It's about creating a habit of turning to God for guidance and strength.

In Ephesians 6:4, fathers are instructed to "bring [their children] up in the training and instruction of the Lord." (Ephesians 6.4, NIV) This is a vital role that fathers play in their children's lives. But you can't lead your children spiritually if your own relationship with God is neglected. Your faith needs to be the foundation of your fatherhood. The truth is, you are never too busy to spend time with God. You can pray during your commute, listen to worship music while working around the house, or read a short passage from the Bible before bed. These small moments add up, nurturing your spiritual life and equipping you to be the father God has called you to be.

Balancing your spiritual growth with the demands of family life may feel like a constant struggle, but God is always with you, offering wisdom and peace. He's not asking for perfection, but for a heart that seeks Him. When you invite God into the daily struggles of fatherhood, you'll find that He provides clarity and direction in ways that make the challenges more manageable. The important thing to remember is that you are not alone. God is present in every season of your life, ready to help you navigate the highs and lows of fatherhood with grace and strength.

Fatherhood is a journey filled with moments of joy, frustration, uncertainty, and growth. But through it all, God remains your source of strength and wisdom. You are doing something incredibly important—not just for your children, but for the kingdom of God. By leading your family in faith, you are planting seeds that will grow into a lasting legacy of spiritual strength. And the more you lean on God, the more equipped you will be to handle the challenges that come your way.

Every day, God offers you the grace and strength to rise to the challenges of fatherhood. As you journey through this devotional, you'll be reminded each week of the biblical principles that can help guide you in your role as a father. It's a reminder that God is not distant or indifferent to your struggles—He is actively working in your life, shaping you to be the father and spiritual leader your family needs.

A Brief Guide on How to Use the Devotional Weekly

This devotional is designed with the busy father in mind, recognizing that between work, family, and personal responsibilities, finding time for spiritual growth can seem like a challenge. The goal is to provide you with weekly reflections, action steps, and prayers that fit into your daily life without overwhelming you. Whether you choose to read it in the morning, during your lunch break, or before bed, each week's devotional is structured to be digestible and impactful.

To get the most out of this devotional, it's helpful to set aside a regular time each week to read the reflection and consider the scripture for the week. This consistency will not only help you grow spiritually but will also set a great example for your children, showing them that your relationship with God is a priority.

Here's a simple guide on how to approach each week:

1. **Start with the Scripture**: Each week begins with a specific passage from the Bible that ties into the theme. Before reading the reflection, take a few moments to read and meditate on the scripture. Ask God to open your heart and mind to what He wants to teach you through His Word. You may even want to read the passage aloud or write it down somewhere you can see it throughout the week as a reminder of the lesson.

2. **Reflect Deeply**: The reflection is designed to address real-life struggles that fathers face, offering biblical wisdom and relatable examples. Take time to engage with the reflection. Ask yourself how the weekly topic relates to your current situation as a father. Are there areas in your life where you feel

the weight of the struggle mentioned? What is God revealing to you through the scripture and reflection? Journaling your thoughts or discussing them with a close friend or spouse can be a helpful way to process what you're learning.

3. **Implement the Action Step**: The action step at the end of each week is not just an add-on—it's a key part of applying what you've read to your life. These are simple, practical steps designed to help you live out the lessons from the week's devotional. They're meant to fit into your daily routine, whether it's taking five minutes in the morning for prayer, initiating a family devotion, or practicing a small habit that helps you lead your family spiritually. Be intentional about completing these steps and revisiting them throughout the week.

4. **Close with Prayer**: Each week concludes with a short prayer that ties together the reflection and action steps. This is your opportunity to invite God into the struggles and victories of your week, asking for His guidance, strength, and wisdom. Feel free to expand on the prayer, making it personal to your specific situation. Prayer is your conversation with God, and it's through prayer that you'll find the strength to grow as a father and spiritual leader.

5. **Daily Bible Readings**: In addition to the weekly reflection, each week includes seven scripture passages—one for each day. These passages are carefully selected to complement the weekly theme and encourage you to spend a few minutes each day in God's Word. You can read these scriptures during your morning routine, during a break, or before bed. It's not about spending hours in study, but rather building a consistent habit of connecting with God daily.

Using the Devotional with Your Family

This devotional can be a powerful tool for not only your personal spiritual growth but also for leading your family in faith. Consider sharing what you're learning with your spouse or children. If your children are old enough, you might choose to incorporate parts of the devotional into family time. Reading a scripture together or praying as a family helps build a strong spiritual foundation for your children and shows them that faith is a vital part of your family's life.

You don't have to go through this devotional alone. If you're part of a men's group at church or have a close circle of friends who are also fathers, you might invite them to go through the devotional with you. Sharing experiences, challenges, and victories with other dads can provide encouragement and accountability. You'll be reminded that fatherhood, with all its joys and struggles, is a journey best walked with God and a supportive community.

Final Thoughts

Remember, this devotional is a journey, not a race. Some weeks may resonate more deeply with you than others, and that's okay. The goal is not to rush through the reflections, but to let God speak to your heart and guide you in becoming the father He has called you to be. Take it one week at a time, trusting that God is working in you and through you to lead your family in faith.

By committing to this devotional, you are making an investment in both your spiritual growth and the spiritual future of your family. It's a reminder that while fatherhood is challenging, it's also one of the most rewarding and important roles you'll ever have. And through it all, you can rest in the knowledge that God is with you every step of the way, offering strength, wisdom, and grace.

The Dad's Faith Guide

A 52-Week Devotional for Christian Dads

Week 1: The Weight of Responsibility

"Come to me, all you who are weary and burdened, and I will give you rest. Take my yoke upon you and learn from me, for I am gentle and humble in heart, and you will find rest for your souls. For my yoke is easy and my burden is light."

(Matthew 11:28-30, NIV)

Daily Bible Reading

Sunday: Matthew 11:28-30	**Thursday**: Proverbs 3:5-6
Monday: 1 Peter 5:7	**Friday**: Philippians 4:6-7
Tuesday: Psalm 55:22	**Saturday**: Psalm 23:1-4
Wednesday: Isaiah 40:31	

Reflection

Fatherhood often brings a deep sense of responsibility, from providing for the family financially to nurturing the emotional and spiritual growth of your children. Many dads find themselves constantly balancing multiple roles—provider, protector, guide, and spiritual leader. With these roles comes an overwhelming pressure to perform, and often, the weight of these expectations can leave fathers feeling exhausted and inadequate. It's easy to reach a point where you feel burdened by the expectations placed on you as a father, but the reality is that God doesn't expect you to carry all of this alone.

Matthew 11:28-30 offers fathers a profound invitation from Jesus: "Come to me, all you who are weary and burdened, and I will give you rest." Jesus understands the demands of life and fatherhood, and He invites you to bring those burdens to Him. He doesn't ask you to shoulder the responsibility of fatherhood on your own. Instead, He offers to help you carry the weight, providing rest for your soul and strength for the tasks ahead. This scripture offers comfort by reminding us that even in our most overwhelming moments, we are not alone—God is present, offering to lift the burden we carry.

As fathers, it's easy to fall into the trap of thinking that we need to do everything ourselves—that every decision, every solution, and every challenge must be handled on our own. But when we lean into God's strength and allow Him to guide us, we can find relief. The call to come to Jesus when we are weary is not a call to laziness or avoiding responsibility. Instead, it's an invitation to shift the weight from our own shoulders onto God's capable hands.

Think of a father who returns home after a long day of work. He's physically tired, emotionally drained, and feels like he's failing at meeting everyone's expectations. His children need attention, his spouse needs support, and the never-ending tasks of life keep piling up. In moments like this, the temptation to push forward out of duty is strong, but that's when the invitation from Jesus becomes most powerful. Rather than trying to push through the exhaustion, He calls us to pause and hand over the weight to Him.

The burden of fatherhood is significant, but it doesn't have to lead to burnout or despair. When you take your burdens to God, He lightens the load. He provides the wisdom and peace needed to handle life's challenges without being consumed by them. In surrendering our need to control everything, we find the rest that only God can give—a rest that recharges our spirit, renews our mind, and allows us to be the fathers God has called us to be.

Action Step

This week, take intentional steps to hand over the specific burdens you've been carrying. Begin by identifying the areas of your life where you feel most overwhelmed—whether it's work responsibilities, financial pressures, parenting challenges, or maintaining your relationship with your spouse. Write these down and commit them to God in prayer. Be specific in your prayer, asking God to take control of these areas and to provide you with the wisdom and strength to handle them.

Another action step is to dedicated five minutes each day for quiet reflection and prayer. This doesn't have to be a long, formal prayer, but rather a moment where you intentionally pause to give God your worries and anxieties. Whether it's in the morning before the day begins or in the evening after your kids go to bed, make it a habit to give your burdens to God. During these moments, remember that God is eager to help and that you don't have to carry everything on your own.

Lastly, consider sharing this burden-lifting practice with your family. Let your children and spouse see that you rely on God's strength and guidance. Set aside a time for family prayer where everyone gets a chance to talk about their day and the challenges they're facing. Together, lift those concerns to God and experience the peace that comes from trusting Him to carry the load.

Closing Prayer

Heavenly Father, I come before You feeling the weight of my responsibilities as a father. There are times when I feel overwhelmed and unsure of how to carry everything I need to. But today, I choose to hand over my burdens to You. Help me to trust You with every aspect of my life—my work, my family, and my own heart. Give me the strength to keep moving forward and the wisdom to know when to rest in Your presence. Teach me to rely on You, knowing that Your yoke is easy and Your burden is light. Walk with me, Lord, as I seek to lead my family in a way that honors You. Amen.

Week 2: Balancing Faith and Family

"There is a time for everything, and a season for every activity under the heavens." (Ecclesiastes 3:1, NIV)

Daily Bible Reading

Sunday: Ecclesiastes 3: 1

Monday: Matthew 6:33

Tuesday: Psalm 90:12

Wednesday: Colossians 3:23

Thursday: James 4:8

Friday: Proverbs 16:9

Saturday: Mark 1:35

Reflection

One of the biggest challenges fathers face is finding time for faith amidst the demands of family life and work. Between providing for your family, attending to your children's needs, and being a supportive partner, your personal spiritual growth can feel like it's slipping away. The busyness of life leaves you feeling stretched thin, and your faith often becomes one more item on an already overflowing to-do list. It's easy to feel guilty about not spending enough time in prayer, Bible study, or reflection, but the reality is that balancing faith and family requires intentional effort.

Ecclesiastes 3:1 reminds us that God has designed life with seasons—there is a time for everything. Just as you make time for family activities, work obligations, and rest, there is also a season for spiritual growth. The beauty of this scripture is that it teaches us not to compartmentalize our faith but to see God's presence in all aspects of life. Balancing faith and family isn't about finding extra time; it's about weaving faith into your everyday moments.

Imagine a typical day: You wake up, help get the kids ready for school, work a full day, come home to more responsibilities, and by the time you hit the pillow, you're exhausted. In the midst of this, finding 30 minutes for Bible study seems impossible. But what if faith became a part of your rhythm, not an additional task? What if you could connect with God during your commute, pray while doing household chores, or reflect on scripture with your family at dinner?

God's design for balance isn't about squeezing Him into the margins of your life but recognizing that He is present in every moment. When you prioritize connecting with God—even in small, consistent ways—your faith becomes the anchor that sustains you. The more you lean into God, the more you'll realize that balance doesn't mean perfection. Some days will be chaotic, and you may not find the quiet time you want, but that doesn't mean you're failing in your faith. It means you're human.

As fathers, the challenge is to model this for our children. When they see you prioritizing time with God, even in the midst of busyness, they learn the importance of relying on Him in all seasons of life. It's not about having a perfect devotional schedule but about showing your family that faith is integral to who you are. Remember, there is a time for everything, and God will guide you through each season, helping you find the balance you seek.

Action Step

This week, focus on incorporating small moments of faith into your daily routine rather than trying to carve out large chunks of time. Here are a few practical steps you can take:

1. **Morning Prayer Routine**: Begin your day with a short prayer before you leave for work or start your morning responsibilities. Even if it's just for two minutes, use this time to thank God for the day ahead and ask for His guidance.
2. **Incorporate Family Devotions**: Choose a specific time during the week to have a short family devotion. This could be at the

dinner table or before bedtime. Read a scripture together, and take turns praying. This helps strengthen not only your faith but also the spiritual bond within your family.

3. **Daily Scripture Reflection**: Pick one verse from the weekly Bible readings and meditate on it throughout the day. Whether it's during a quiet moment or while you're completing daily tasks, let that verse guide your thoughts and actions.

By integrating these small habits into your busy schedule, you'll find that faith becomes a natural part of your routine, allowing you to grow spiritually even in the midst of life's demands.

Closing Prayer

Heavenly Father, I come to You today feeling the weight of balancing my responsibilities as a father, husband, and provider. There are moments when I struggle to find time for You, but I know that You are with me in every season. Help me to see Your presence in the everyday moments of my life. Teach me to lean on You for strength, and show me how to make time for spiritual growth even when life is busy. Guide me as I lead my family in faith and help me to be an example of Your love and grace. Amen.

Week 3: Leading by Example

"Follow my example, as I follow the example of Christ."
(1 Corinthians 11:1, NIV)

Daily Bible Reading

Sunday: 1 Corinthians 11:1	**Thursday**: 1 Peter 5:3
Monday: Proverbs 22:6	**Friday**: Matthew 5:14-16
Tuesday: Ephesians 5:1-2	**Saturday**: Philippians 4:9
Wednesday: Titus 2:7-8	

Reflection

One of the deepest challenges for fathers is the pressure to be a role model for their children when they feel far from perfect. It's easy to look at the areas where you fall short and feel inadequate. As fathers, you want to lead your children well, guiding them in faith, values, and life decisions, but what do you do when you feel like you're failing in some of those areas yourself?

The truth is, none of us are perfect. But 1 Corinthians 11:1 provides a powerful reminder: "Follow my example, as I follow the example of Christ." This scripture doesn't call us to be flawless role models. Instead, it invites us to model our lives on Christ and demonstrate what it looks like to humbly pursue God, even through our imperfections.

Being a father is not about having everything figured out; it's about showing your children what it means to seek God in all things, including your weaknesses. When you model humility, growth, and a willingness to learn from mistakes, you show your children that the Christian life is about grace and continual transformation. You don't have to be a perfect father—you are called to be a faithful one.

Consider how powerful it is for your children to see you admit when you've made a mistake and to witness you actively working on that area of your life. Perhaps you've had moments where your temper flared or you made a decision you regret. When you go to your children and say, "I didn't handle that well, but I'm working on it, and I'm asking God to help me," you are modeling a life of grace, repentance, and dependence on God.

Children are not expecting perfection from their fathers. What they need to see is your example of humility, growth, and faith. Let them see you praying when you're stressed, turning to scripture for guidance, and asking for forgiveness when necessary. By doing so, you're teaching them that life with Christ is not about having it all together, but about allowing Him to guide you, even when you don't.

The beauty of leading by example is that your children are learning not only through your successes but also through your struggles. When they see you walking through a difficult season with faith, they learn resilience. When they see you working on areas of your life that need improvement, they learn perseverance. And when they see you growing in your walk with God, they learn the value of a lifelong journey of faith.

As you reflect on being a role model for your children, remember that the best example you can set is one that points them toward Christ. When they see you striving to follow Jesus, even in your imperfections, they'll learn that following God is not about being perfect, but about faithfully walking in His grace.

Action Step

This week, take a step toward leading by example in a specific area of your life. Choose one area where you know you can improve for the sake of your children. It could be something like managing your temper, spending more intentional time with them, or showing more patience in your interactions. Whatever it is, make a conscious effort to work on it this week, with God's help.

Here are some practical steps you can take:

1. **Reflect and Pray**: Take a few moments to pray and ask God to reveal the area where He wants you to grow. Be honest with yourself about where you've fallen short, and invite God to give you the strength to improve in that area.
2. **Involve Your Children**: Depending on the age of your children, you may want to share with them the specific area you're working on. This transparency can be powerful in showing them that even adults continue to grow and learn.
3. **Daily Accountability**: Keep track of your progress by checking in with yourself each day. You may want to journal briefly at the end of each day, reflecting on how you handled situations where you needed improvement. Offer the day's successes and failures to God in prayer, asking Him to continue guiding you in this journey of growth.

By focusing on one specific area and inviting God to help you improve, you're not only growing yourself but also setting a powerful example for your children to follow.

Closing Prayer

Heavenly Father, I come to You recognizing my imperfections as a father. There are moments when I fall short, and I struggle to be the example that my children need. But I thank You for Your grace and for the reminder that I don't have to be perfect—I just need to follow You. Help me, Lord, to model humility and growth for my children. Teach me to lead by example, even when it means showing them my weaknesses. Give me the wisdom and strength to improve in the areas where I fall short, and let my life point them toward You. Guide me as I strive to follow Christ's example, and may my children see Your love and grace reflected in my life. Amen.

Week 4: Overcoming Fatherly Doubts

"If any of you lacks wisdom, you should ask God, who gives generously to all without finding fault, and it will be given to you." (James 1:5, NIV)

Daily Bible Reading

Sunday: James 1:5

Monday: Proverbs 3:5-6

Tuesday: Philippians 4:6-7

Wednesday: Psalm 32:8

Thursday: Proverbs 16:9

Friday: Isaiah 41:10

Saturday: Psalm 34:17-18

Reflection

As a father, it's natural to sometimes question whether you're doing enough or if you're getting it right. You might wonder if the decisions you make are really the best for your children. Are you teaching them the right values? Are you showing enough love, or are you too tough or too lenient? These questions can lead to doubts that weigh heavily on your heart. The pressure to be a good father can feel overwhelming, especially when you feel like you're falling short.

Doubting your ability to be a good father is a struggle that most dads will face at some point. It's easy to compare yourself to other fathers or feel inadequate when you make mistakes. But the Bible gives us a reassuring promise in James 1:5: "If any of you lacks wisdom, you should ask God, who gives generously to all without finding fault, and it will be given to you." This verse is a reminder that when we feel uncertain, we don't have to rely on our own understanding. God is always there to provide the wisdom we need.

Fatherhood isn't about having all the answers. It's about relying on God to guide you through the journey. When you're faced with difficult decisions, or when doubts creep in, you can turn to God in prayer and ask for His wisdom. He promises to give it generously, without judgment. God understands the weight of the responsibility you carry, and He is ready to help you navigate it.

Consider a father who feels unsure about how to discipline his children. He worries that he's either being too strict or too lenient, and he fears that his decisions may negatively impact them. In moments like these, the weight of doubt can be heavy, leading to second-guessing every choice. But James 1:5 provides comfort: God is ready to give the wisdom needed in that situation. When we approach Him in humility, acknowledging our need for His guidance, He will respond.

Parenting involves countless decisions, and it's easy to feel overwhelmed by the responsibility of getting it right. But God's wisdom is available to you whenever you ask. Rather than letting doubts paralyze you, trust that God is working through you. Your role as a father is not to be perfect but to be faithful. Faithfulness includes seeking God's help when you don't know what to do, trusting that He will direct your steps.

Doubt may make you feel isolated, but remember that God is with you in every decision. He understands your fears and your concerns. As you seek His wisdom, He will provide clarity and peace. You're not expected to be flawless, but you are called to rely on the One who is.

Action Step

This week, take time to address your doubts by writing them down and bringing them to God in prayer. Start by identifying specific areas where you feel unsure or inadequate as a father. Do you worry about making the right choices in disciplining your children? Do you struggle to balance time between work and family? Are you uncertain about how to lead your family spiritually?

Once you've identified these doubts, commit them to God in prayer. Use James 1:5 as a foundation for your prayers, asking God to give you the wisdom and clarity you need in each area. As you pray, remember that God promises to give generously to those who seek His guidance.

Additionally, take a practical step by discussing one of your doubts with your spouse or a trusted friend. Sometimes talking through your concerns with someone else can bring fresh perspective and remind you that you're not alone in this journey.

Lastly, make it a habit to ask God for wisdom daily. You don't need to wait until you're overwhelmed by doubt. Begin each day by acknowledging your need for God's guidance, and trust that He will lead you as you navigate the challenges of fatherhood.

Closing Prayer

Heavenly Father, I come to You with the doubts and fears that weigh on my heart as a father. There are moments when I feel unsure of my decisions and inadequate in my role. But I thank You for Your promise in James 1:5 that if I lack wisdom, I can come to You, and You will give it generously. Lord, I ask for Your wisdom and guidance in the areas where I feel uncertain. Help me to trust that You are leading me, even when I don't have all the answers. Teach me to rely on Your strength and not my own. I pray that You give me peace and clarity in my decisions, and that through my faithfulness, my children may see Your love and grace. In Jesus' name, Amen.

Week 5: The Challenges of Discipline

"No discipline seems pleasant at the time, but painful. Later on, however, it produces a harvest of righteousness and peace for those who have been trained by it." (Hebrews 12:11, NIV)

Daily Bible Reading

Sunday: Hebrews 12:11

Monday: Proverbs 13:24

Tuesday: Ephesians 6:4

Wednesday: Colossians 3:21

Thursday: Proverbs 3:11-12

Friday: James 1:19-20

Saturday: Proverbs 19:18

Reflection

As fathers, one of the most difficult roles we play is that of a disciplinarian. We want our children to grow up knowing right from wrong, but we also don't want to push them away with harshness. Discipline is essential for guiding our children, but balancing it with grace can often feel like walking a tightrope. It's easy to react out of frustration, especially after a long day, or when repeated disobedience tests your patience. In these moments, discipline can quickly turn into anger, and the balance between correction and compassion is lost.

Hebrews 12:11 reminds us that discipline is not pleasant, neither for the child nor for the parent. It's painful at times, but it is necessary. The verse continues to assure us that, over time, discipline produces a "harvest of righteousness and peace." This scripture helps us understand that discipline, when done correctly and with love, is not merely about punishment. It is about teaching, guiding, and ultimately producing character and righteousness in our children.

When disciplining your children, it's important to remember that your goal is not to control them but to shape their hearts. This is where balancing discipline with grace becomes crucial. Just as God disciplines us out of love to guide us toward righteousness, we are called to do the same for our children. However, discipline must always be rooted in love and must reflect God's grace toward us.

Consider a scenario where your child disobeys repeatedly, and you find yourself losing patience. In that moment, the temptation to react in anger is strong. But if you step back, pray, and ask God for wisdom, you can discipline out of love instead of frustration. The difference between disciplining in anger and disciplining with grace is significant. Anger can damage your relationship with your child and leave them feeling ashamed or disconnected. Discipline rooted in love, however, leads to growth and understanding.

One real-life challenge that many fathers face is wondering if they're being too hard on their children or, conversely, too lenient. If discipline is too harsh, children may become resentful or fearful. If it's too soft, they may not learn important lessons about responsibility and consequences. This is where trusting God's wisdom comes into play. He can guide you to discern when to be firm and when to extend grace, always remembering that both discipline and grace must work together.

Jesus modeled this balance for us. When He corrected His disciples, He did so in love, not to shame them, but to lead them toward truth. He offered forgiveness when needed but never shied away from correcting wrong behavior. As fathers, we are called to follow this example—disciplining with love, but not abandoning grace.

The reality is that discipline will always be one of the hardest parts of parenting. But by seeking God's wisdom and reflecting on His example, you can find the balance between correction and compassion. Your children need structure and consequences, but they also need to feel loved and supported, even when they make mistakes. Discipline that is done in love and paired with grace will lead to the peace and righteousness God promises.

Action Step

This week, take time to reflect on your approach to discipline. Consider the last time you disciplined your child—was it done in love, or was it fueled by frustration? Write down what happened and examine your response. Did it reflect the grace and patience of God? If not, bring that moment to God in prayer, asking for wisdom to handle future situations with more balance.

Here are some practical steps you can take this week:

1. **Pray Before Acting**: The next time you find yourself needing to discipline your child, pause and pray before responding. Ask God for patience and wisdom to guide your actions so that your discipline reflects love and not anger.
2. **Evaluate the Situation with Your Child**: After disciplining your child, take a moment to explain why you had to correct them. Help them understand the reason behind the discipline and remind them of your love for them. This helps reinforce that discipline is for their growth, not out of frustration or anger.
3. **Establish a Consistent Approach**: Consistency is key when balancing discipline with grace. Ensure that your discipline is not arbitrary or emotionally driven. Set clear expectations with your children and establish consistent consequences that are both fair and loving.

Closing Prayer

Heavenly Father, I come before You seeking wisdom in how I discipline my children. I know that discipline is necessary, but I often struggle to balance it with grace. Help me to correct my children in love, just as You lovingly guide me. Teach me to be patient and to lead by example, reflecting Your grace and truth in every action. When I feel frustrated, remind me to pause and seek Your wisdom. Lord, I ask that You help me to raise my children in a way that honors You, shaping their hearts toward righteousness and peace. Thank You for being a perfect example of how to lead with love and discipline. In Jesus' name, Amen.

Week 6: Teaching Patience in a Fast-Paced World

"But the fruit of the Spirit is love, joy, peace, forbearance, kindness, goodness, faithfulness, gentleness and self-control. Against such things there is no law." (Galatians 5:22-23, NIV)

Daily Bible Reading

Sunday: Galatians 5:22-23

Monday: Colossians 3:12

Tuesday: 1 Corinthians 13:4-5

Wednesday: Ephesians 4:2

Thursday: Psalm 37:7

Friday: James 1:19

Saturday: Proverbs 14:29

Reflection

In today's fast-paced world, patience can feel like a distant virtue. Everywhere we turn, we're conditioned for speed—whether it's through technology, instant gratification, or the expectation to keep up with life's demands. As fathers, this often affects how we handle our children's behavior and growth. When they're not learning as quickly as we'd like or repeating mistakes we thought they'd outgrown, our patience can wear thin. It's easy to become frustrated or feel that they aren't progressing at the pace we expect.

But Galatians 5:22-23 reminds us that patience, or "forbearance," is a fruit of the Spirit. It's not something we naturally have an endless supply of—it's something that grows as we walk with God and allow His Spirit to guide us. The patience that God calls us to extend toward our children isn't a product of our own effort; it is a reflection of the patience He shows us daily. Just as God is slow to anger and abounding in love toward us, we are called to demonstrate that same patience toward our children as they grow, make mistakes, and learn.

Consider how God responds to our failures. He is never rushed, never impatient with our growth. He sees our potential and knows that growth takes time. When we fail, He gently corrects us and leads us back on the right path. Similarly, our role as fathers is not to rush our children's development but to guide them with the same patience God shows us. This means allowing room for their mistakes, being slow to anger, and offering grace when they fall short.

Imagine a scenario where your child is struggling to follow directions or to learn a new skill. The temptation to become irritated or to respond harshly can be strong, especially when life feels hectic. But responding with patience in that moment can make all the difference. It not only teaches your child that it's okay to make mistakes, but it also shows them that they are valued for who they are, not just for what they can do.

The reality is that fatherhood will constantly challenge your patience. There will be days when your children test your limits, but those are the moments when God calls you to lean on Him. When you feel your patience slipping, take a step back and remember how patient God has been with you. Reflect on the times when you needed extra grace and how He lovingly extended it to you. Let that understanding fuel the way you respond to your children.

Patience with your children isn't about letting things slide or avoiding correction; it's about correcting in love and giving them the space to grow at their own pace. It's about meeting them where they are and trusting that, with time and guidance, they will become who God has created them to be. Just as a gardener patiently waits for a seed to grow into a full plant, trusting the process even when it's slow, fathers are called to patiently nurture their children's development, trusting God with the outcome.

In a world that pushes for quick results and perfection, teaching patience to our children starts with us modeling it in our own behavior. When we choose patience, we are teaching them that growth takes time, and that love is not conditional on performance. And in doing so, we point them toward the ultimate source of patience—God Himself.

Action Step

This week, focus on practicing moments of patience, especially when it's most difficult. Here are some practical steps you can take:

1. **Pause Before Reacting**: The next time your child tests your patience, take a moment to pause before responding. In that pause, offer a quick prayer asking God to help you respond with grace rather than frustration. This simple pause can make a significant difference in how you handle the situation.
2. **Set Realistic Expectations**: Reflect on whether your expectations for your child's behavior or growth are realistic. Children develop at different rates, and some skills or behaviors take time to learn. Adjust your expectations if needed, and give your child the grace to grow at their own pace.
3. **Practice Patience in Front of Your Child**: Let your child see you exercising patience, whether it's with them, with another family member, or even in a frustrating situation like waiting in traffic. Use these moments as teaching opportunities to explain how patience can help us navigate life with more peace and kindness.

By taking these small steps, you'll not only grow in patience yourself but also model this vital fruit of the Spirit for your children, showing them how to be patient with others and with themselves.

Closing Prayer

Heavenly Father, thank You for the patience You show me each day. I recognize how often I fall short and how much I need Your grace. Lord, help me to extend that same patience to my children. Teach me to be slow to anger and quick to listen, just as You are with me. When I'm tempted to react out of frustration, remind me to pause and reflect on Your love. Guide me as I teach my children with patience, trusting You with their growth. Let my actions reflect Your heart so that my children can see Your love through me. Help me to model the fruit of the Spirit in my home and to lead with grace. In Jesus' name, Amen.

Week 7: Building Trust with Your Children

"Let love and faithfulness never leave you; bind them around your neck, write them on the tablet of your heart. Then you will win favor and a good name in the sight of God and man."

(Proverbs 3:3-4, NIV)

Daily Bible Reading

Sunday: Proverbs 3:3-4
Monday: Colossians 3:9-10
Tuesday: Ephesians 4:15
Wednesday: 1 Thessalonians 5:11

Thursday: Matthew 5:37
Friday: Psalm 25:4-5
Saturday: James 5:12

Reflection

Trust is one of the foundational elements of any relationship, especially the relationship between a father and his children. It's easy to take for granted the importance of trust, assuming that because you're the parent, trust comes automatically. However, the reality is that trust must be earned and, perhaps more importantly, maintained over time. As your children grow, they will look to you as their guide, protector, and confidant. If they can trust you, they will feel safe and secure in your leadership. But if trust is broken, it can be difficult to repair.

Proverbs 3:3-4 teaches us that trust is built on love and faithfulness. When your children know that you love them unconditionally and that you are consistent in your words and actions, they will naturally place their trust in you. Trust is not about perfection; it's about reliability. Your children need to know that they can count on you to be honest with them, to keep your promises, and to act with their best interests at heart.

One common struggle many fathers face is earning their children's trust after it has been damaged. Perhaps you made a promise that you couldn't keep, or maybe you reacted harshly in a moment of frustration. While these moments don't define you as a father, they can create small cracks in the foundation of trust. The good news is that trust can be rebuilt through consistent actions of love, honesty, and humility.

Children are quick to forgive, but they need to see that you are trustworthy. This means acknowledging when you make mistakes and being willing to apologize. If you've ever been in a situation where your reaction was too harsh or you failed to follow through on a promise, the first step toward rebuilding trust is to own your actions. Your children don't expect you to be perfect, but they do expect you to be honest.

Imagine a father who, due to work commitments, promised to spend time with his child but had to cancel multiple times. Over time, the child may begin to feel like they are not a priority. While the father's intentions were good, his actions have sent a different message. To rebuild that trust, the father needs to be intentional about keeping his word in the future and making time for his child, even if it requires some sacrifice.

Trust is also built in the little moments—being present during family conversations, listening intently to your children's concerns, and showing them that they can rely on you. These consistent, everyday actions build a foundation of trust that will last. Your children need to know that they can come to you with their struggles, fears, and questions, and that you will respond with love and understanding, not judgment.

As fathers, one of the most important ways we build trust is by modeling integrity. This means being truthful in all circumstances, even when it's difficult or uncomfortable. When your children see that you are a man of your word, they will learn to trust not only you but also the values you are instilling in them.

Trust takes time to build, but once established, it can form a strong bond between you and your children that will last a lifetime. As you continue to walk in love, faithfulness, and honesty, you will see that trust grows naturally.

Action Step

This week, focus on taking practical steps to build or strengthen trust with your children. Here are a few actionable ideas you can implement:

1. **Have an Open Conversation**: Take time this week to have an honest, heart-to-heart conversation with your child. Ask them how they feel about your relationship and whether there's anything they think you could improve on as their father. Listen without interrupting and assure them that their thoughts and feelings are important to you. This will open up opportunities for trust to grow.
2. **Keep Your Word**: If you make a promise this week, no matter how small, make sure to keep it. Whether it's a promise to spend time together or help with homework, let your children see that they can rely on your word. Consistency in following through builds trust over time.
3. **Apologize When Needed**: If you've made mistakes or broken trust in the past, take time to acknowledge those moments. Apologizing to your children is not a sign of weakness, but a demonstration of humility and love. It teaches them that even when we fall short, we can always seek reconciliation and restoration.

By taking these steps, you'll create an environment of trust where your children feel valued, heard, and secure in their relationship with you.

Closing Prayer

Heavenly Father, thank You for the gift of trust and the relationships You've given me with my children. I know that trust is a precious thing, and I ask for Your wisdom as I strive to build and maintain that trust with them. Help me to walk in love, consistency, and faithfulness, just as You have shown me. When I fall short, give me the humility to apologize and the grace to rebuild what has been broken. Guide me to be a father they can rely on, and let my actions reflect Your love in every moment. Lord, I pray that as I seek to earn and maintain their trust, they will also learn to trust You as their heavenly Father. In Jesus' name, Amen.

Week 8: Protecting Your Family's Spiritual Health

"But if serving the Lord seems undesirable to you, then choose for yourselves this day whom you will serve, whether the gods your ancestors served beyond the Euphrates, or the gods of the Amorites, in whose land you are living. But as for me and my household, we will serve the Lord." (Joshua 24:15, NIV)

Daily Bible Reading

Sunday: Joshua 24:15

Monday: Ephesians 6:4

Tuesday: Deuteronomy 6:6-7

Wednesday: Matthew 6:33

Thursday: Proverbs 22:6

Friday: Psalm 127:1-2

Saturday: Colossians 3:16

Reflection

As fathers, we are called to protect our families, not just physically but spiritually as well. In today's world, where distractions abound and external influences pull at every corner of life, safeguarding our family's spiritual health becomes one of our most critical responsibilities. Whether it's the constant noise of social media, the allure of materialism, or conflicting cultural values, these forces threaten to divert our focus away from God and toward worldly pursuits. In this environment, fathers have a unique and essential role in guiding their families toward a strong, unwavering commitment to serving the Lord.

Joshua's declaration in Joshua 24:15 is a powerful call to action. He makes a public and personal stand, boldly proclaiming that no matter what distractions or influences are present, his household will serve the Lord. This scripture emphasizes the father's responsibility to take a leadership role in the spiritual direction of the family. It's not a passive commitment—it's an intentional, daily choice to make God the center of your home.

The distractions that threaten your family's spiritual health are real, and often subtle. It might not always be obvious when something is pulling your children or spouse away from God, but over time, these influences can weaken your family's spiritual foundation. As a father, you need to be vigilant and proactive in creating an environment where God's Word, prayer, and faith are at the center of family life.

Imagine the scenario of a father who works long hours, spends his weekends watching sports, and finds little time to engage his family in spiritual practices. Over time, his children may begin to prioritize entertainment, school, or friends over their relationship with God because they don't see their father modeling a life of faith. This isn't intentional neglect, but without a conscious effort to lead spiritually, the family's focus can drift toward worldly things.

On the other hand, consider a father who makes time each day to pray with his family, who reads scripture at the dinner table, and who sets aside time each week for a family devotional. His children see, through his consistent actions, that faith is not just something reserved for Sundays but is woven into the fabric of their daily lives. These moments of spiritual investment help shield the family from the distractions and influences of the world, grounding them in the truth of God's Word.

Being a spiritual leader in your home doesn't mean you have to have all the answers or be perfect in your faith journey. It means making a commitment to prioritize God in your household and guiding your family in that direction, even when life is busy or challenging. It's about being intentional with your time, showing your children through example that serving the Lord is the highest priority. Your family will learn from what you model—how you handle stress, how you make decisions, and how you relate to God in both the good and tough times.

The reality is that the world will always have distractions. But when you take an active role in guiding your family spiritually, you create a shield of protection that can withstand the pressures of the world. As Joshua declared, "As for me and my household, we will serve the Lord." This is not just a one-time declaration, but a daily commitment to protect your family's spiritual health by intentionally focusing on God in every aspect of life.

Action Step

This week, focus on creating a rhythm of spiritual practices that will strengthen your family's spiritual health. Here are three practical steps you can take to start:

1. **Create a Family Prayer Time**: Set aside a specific time each day for your family to pray together. This could be in the morning before the day begins, at the dinner table, or before bed. Make this a non-negotiable time where your family gathers to pray for each other, give thanks, and ask for God's guidance in your lives.
2. **Initiate a Bible Reading Session**: Choose a day each week where your family reads a chapter or a passage from the Bible together. Discuss how the scripture applies to your family's current circumstances. Encourage your children to ask questions and share their thoughts. This builds a habit of seeking God's Word as a guide for life.
3. **Limit Distractions**: Identify one distraction that often pulls your family away from spending time with God—whether it's too much screen time, busy schedules, or extracurricular activities. This week, commit to reducing or eliminating that distraction and replace it with a family activity that brings you

closer to God, such as going for a walk and discussing His creation or sharing what you're thankful for.

By taking these steps, you'll be actively protecting your family's spiritual health and ensuring that God remains at the center of your home.

Closing Prayer

Heavenly Father, I thank You for the gift of my family and the responsibility You've given me to lead them toward You. In a world full of distractions and influences that can pull us away from You, I ask for Your wisdom and strength. Help me to guide my family in truth, to prioritize You above all else, and to protect our spiritual health. Lord, give me the courage to stand firm like Joshua, declaring that we will serve You, no matter what the world offers. Let our home be a place where Your Word is honored, and Your presence is felt every day. Guard us from the distractions that threaten to pull us away from You, and help us to grow closer to You as a family. In Jesus' name, Amen.

Week 9: Trusting God with Your Children's Future

"For I know the plans I have for you," declares the Lord, "plans to prosper you and not to harm you, plans to give you hope and a future." (Jeremiah 29:11, NIV)

<table><tr><td colspan="2" align="center">Daily Bible Reading</td></tr><tr><td>Sunday: Jeremiah 29:11</td><td>Thursday: Philippians 4:6-7</td></tr><tr><td>Monday: Proverbs 16:9</td><td>Friday: Isaiah 41:10</td></tr><tr><td>Tuesday: Psalm 37:5</td><td>Saturday: Psalm 121:7-8</td></tr><tr><td>Wednesday: Matthew 6:25-27</td><td></td></tr></table>

Reflection

As a father, one of the deepest and most constant concerns you may carry is about your children's future. Will they be safe, happy, and secure? Are you preparing them well for the challenges they will face in life? These questions can fill your heart with anxiety, especially in a world that often feels unpredictable and out of control. You want to protect them from harm and guide them toward a successful future, but many things are beyond your control. The struggle to let go of these concerns and trust God with your children's future can be overwhelming.

Jeremiah 29:11 gives us a powerful reminder of God's sovereignty and goodness. God promises that He has plans for us, plans for good and not for harm, plans to give us hope and a future. While this verse was spoken to the Israelites during a difficult time in their history, it speaks to the timeless truth that God's plans for His people are full of hope. As a father, this truth also applies to your children. God has a plan for their lives, and it is a plan that is good. He sees what you cannot, and He knows what they will need long before you do.

The challenge for fathers is learning to trust in God's plan over your own. As much as you want to control every aspect of your child's life, there will be times when you must release them into God's hands. Perhaps it's when they're starting school, making friends, or making important life decisions. Each stage of their life will present new challenges and uncertainties, but God is with them through it all.

Imagine a father whose child is struggling in school, and he begins to worry about how this will affect their future. Will they ever catch up? Will this hurt their self-esteem? Will they have opportunities to succeed? It's easy to spiral into a cycle of anxiety when things don't seem to be going well. However, in moments like these, the key is to remember that God is working in their lives in ways you can't always see. Your role is to provide guidance and support, but ultimately, their future is in God's hands.

It's important to realize that while your influence as a father is significant, God's guidance is greater. He sees the entire path ahead for your children. He knows their strengths, weaknesses, and potential. When you trust God with your children's future, you release the burden of trying to control everything and instead place them into the loving, all-knowing hands of their Creator.

This doesn't mean that you stop caring or stop guiding them. Rather, it means that as you lead them, you do so with the peace that comes from knowing God is in control. It's about balancing your responsibility as a father with the understanding that God is the ultimate Father. He loves your children even more than you do, and His plans for them are filled with hope.

The reality is that there will always be moments of doubt and fear when it comes to your children's future. But in those moments, remember that God's plans are bigger than your worries. His promises are true, and He will never leave your children or forsake them. Trusting in Him is the greatest gift you can give to both yourself and your children.

Action Step

This week, take intentional steps to hand over your anxieties about your children's future to God. Here are some practical actions to help you apply this lesson:

1. **Write Down Your Concerns**: Take a few moments to write down the specific concerns you have about each of your children's futures. Whether it's related to their education, friendships, health, or spiritual growth, name the worries that weigh on your heart. Once you've written them down, bring them to God in prayer, asking Him to take control and to give you peace as you trust Him with their future.
2. **Pray Daily for Your Children**: Set aside a specific time each day to pray for your children, asking God to guide them and protect them. This could be during your morning routine, in the evening before bed, or even during a quiet moment at work. The more you pray, the more you will feel the peace of God replacing your anxiety with trust.
3. **Create a Family Prayer Time**: Involve your children in the process of trusting God by creating a family prayer time or

Bible reading session. This helps instill in them the importance of relying on God for their future. During this time, you can openly discuss your hopes and dreams for them, but also model what it looks like to surrender those dreams to God's will.

By taking these steps, you'll find that your worries are replaced with confidence in God's promises. You'll also be teaching your children an invaluable lesson—how to trust God with their own lives.

Closing Prayer

Heavenly Father, I come to You with the concerns and fears I have about my children's future. I love them so deeply and want the best for them, but I know that my control is limited. Today, I place their futures into Your capable hands. Lord, I trust that You have good plans for them, plans to give them hope and a future, as You promised in Jeremiah 29:11. Help me to release my anxieties and trust in Your perfect wisdom and timing. Guide my children, protect them, and lead them on the path You have prepared for them. Give me peace as I trust You, knowing that You are always with them. Thank You for loving my children even more than I do, and for being the ultimate Father who knows what they need before I do. In Jesus' name, Amen.

Week 10: Overcoming Loneliness and Depression as a Father

"The Lord is close to the brokenhearted and saves those who are crushed in spirit." (Psalm 34:18, NIV)

Daily Bible Reading

Sunday: Psalm 34:18

Monday: Matthew 11:28-30

Tuesday: 1 Peter 5:7

Wednesday: Isaiah 41:10

Thursday: Romans 8:38-39

Friday: 2 Corinthians 12:9

Saturday: Psalm 147:3

Reflection

As a father, the responsibility to care for your family can feel overwhelming at times, especially when battling feelings of loneliness and depression. These emotions may arise from various sources—unspoken struggles, the pressures of providing for your family, or feeling disconnected despite the busyness of life. It can be difficult to admit to these feelings because society often expects men, particularly fathers, to be strong and composed. Yet, even the strongest father can feel isolated and burdened by the weight of his role.

Psalm 34:18 offers comfort in these moments of loneliness and despair, reminding us that God is close to those who are brokenhearted. He understands our struggles, even the ones we may not be able to share with others. Depression often isolates, making fathers feel as though they are fighting battles alone. However, God is present, offering His comfort and healing for those crushed in spirit.

One of the emotional challenges fathers face is the pressure to appear invulnerable for their families, leaving little room to address their own feelings of loneliness. Depression doesn't always look like sadness; it can manifest in irritability, fatigue, and a sense of emotional numbness. Fathers may feel disconnected from their spouses, children, or friends, leading to deeper feelings of isolation.

The practical challenge comes in seeking help or opening up about these struggles. As a father, it's natural to want to solve problems independently, but God calls us to cast our burdens onto Him (1 Peter 5:7). By turning to God in prayer, fathers can find a source of strength and hope in moments of deep despair.

It's important to recognize that depression and loneliness are not signs of failure, but rather, they are human experiences. Trusting in God's promise to never leave or forsake us (Isaiah 41:10) can provide a foundation of hope. His presence offers comfort and peace even in the darkest moments. Opening up to others—whether through a trusted friend, counselor, or pastor—can also bring light into a father's struggle with loneliness. Seeking support is not a sign of weakness but a step toward healing.

God is near, and He calls fathers to rest in His grace, reminding them that they are not alone.

Action Steps

1. **Reach Out for Support:** Take a moment to reflect on someone you trust—whether it's a friend, your spouse, or a pastor—and reach out to share what you're going through. It's often difficult to admit to feelings of loneliness or depression, but simply talking to someone can lighten the emotional load.

Remember that God placed people in your life to offer support, and being vulnerable with others is a way to start the healing process.

2. **Turn to God in Prayer**: When feelings of loneliness or depression start to take hold, take a moment to turn to God in prayer. Speak openly with Him about what you're feeling, even if the emotions are hard to put into words. Trust that He hears you and is near to those who are hurting. Use this time to release your burdens to Him, knowing that He can provide the peace and comfort that surpasses understanding.

3. **Prioritize Your Mental and Emotional Well-being**: Take small, intentional steps to care for your mental and emotional health. Whether that means setting aside time each day for quiet reflection, journaling your thoughts, or scheduling an appointment with a counselor, prioritize activities that help you process your emotions. You can't pour from an empty cup, so ensuring that you are emotionally healthy will allow you to better care for your family.

By reaching out to others, praying, and prioritizing your mental health, you can begin to heal from the effects of loneliness and depression. Remember, you don't have to carry these burdens alone—God is with you, and there are people ready to support you.

Closing Prayer

Heavenly Father, Thank You for always being near to the brokenhearted and for offering comfort to those crushed in spirit. I come before You, Lord, asking for Your help in my moments of loneliness and depression. You see the burdens I carry, even the ones I struggle to express, and I trust that You are walking with me through this difficult season.

Grant me the strength to open up to others and seek the support I need. Help me to remember that I am never truly alone because You are always with me. Renew my spirit and fill me with Your peace that transcends understanding. Guide me as I navigate these emotions, and help me to find rest in You.

Thank You for being my constant source of strength. I place my worries and my heartache in Your hands, trusting that You will carry me through.

In Jesus' name, I pray. Amen.

Week 11: Overcoming Personal Failures

"Therefore, there is now no condemnation for those who are in Christ Jesus." (Romans 8:1, NIV)

Daily Bible Reading

Sunday: Romans 8:1

Monday: 1 John 1:9

Tuesday: Psalm 103:10-12

Wednesday: 2 Corinthians 12:9-10

Thursday: Micah 7:18-19

Friday: Isaiah 43:18-19

Saturday: Colossians 3:13

Reflection

Fatherhood brings many moments of joy, but it also comes with its share of mistakes and failures. As a father, you've likely experienced times when you've fallen short—whether it's through a harsh word spoken in anger, a broken promise, or a situation where you felt inadequate to meet your child's needs. The weight of these failures can be heavy, often leading to feelings of guilt and shame. You may question if you're doing enough or if you're capable of being the father your children deserve.

Romans 8:1 provides an important truth that can help you navigate these moments of failure: "Therefore, there is now no condemnation for those who are in Christ Jesus." This scripture is a powerful reminder that even in our failures, God's grace covers us. When we turn to Him in repentance, He forgives us and releases us from the burden of guilt. You don't need to carry the weight of your past mistakes because, in Christ, you are free from condemnation.

But as much as we understand God's forgiveness in theory, it can be difficult to apply it to our own lives as fathers. You might still wrestle with guilt, replaying moments where you could have done things differently. You might worry about how your mistakes have impacted your children, wondering if they'll remember your shortcomings more than your love.

It's important to recognize that God's grace isn't just theoretical—it's active and available in your daily life. God doesn't hold your failures against you, and neither should you. Instead of allowing guilt to paralyze you, lean into God's grace. Acknowledge where you've made mistakes, but also accept that you are a work in progress, just as your children are.

Imagine a father who feels he's failed because he missed several important moments in his child's life due to work commitments. He carries that guilt with him, worrying that his child will feel unloved or neglected. But when he turns to God and asks for forgiveness, he's reminded that God's grace is bigger than his mistakes. He can choose to use those past failures as opportunities for growth, committing to being more present in the future.

This doesn't mean that your mistakes don't matter—of course, it's important to learn from them and seek to grow. But God's grace allows you to move forward without being defined by those failures. As a father, one of the greatest lessons you can teach your children is how to handle mistakes. By showing them that failure isn't the end of the story, but a chance to lean on God's strength and forgiveness, you model humility and resilience.

God's grace is a reminder that you don't have to be a perfect father, only a faithful one. He's not asking for perfection—He's asking for trust and reliance on Him. Your children will see your love for them, not just in your successes, but in how you handle your shortcomings. When you acknowledge your mistakes, seek forgiveness, and commit to doing better, you demonstrate the very grace that God extends to all of us.

Action Step

Here are some practical steps you can take this week to overcome the weight of personal failures and embrace God's grace:

1. **Forgive Yourself for a Past Mistake**: Think about a specific mistake or failure that has weighed on you as a father. It could be something recent or something from years ago. Write it down and acknowledge it before God. Then, ask for His forgiveness and, most importantly, forgive yourself. As you release this burden, remember Romans 8:1—there is no condemnation for those who are in Christ.

2. **Have an Honest Conversation with Your Children**: If your failure involved your children—whether it was a broken promise, harsh words, or being absent—take time to talk with them about it. Apologize where necessary and let them know how much you love them. This teaches them that it's okay to admit mistakes and that relationships can be strengthened through honesty and grace.

3. **Create a Family Prayer Time**: Gather your family and pray together, focusing on the theme of grace and forgiveness. During this time, invite your children to share any burdens or worries they might have, and model how to bring those concerns to God. This creates a space where your children feel safe and supported, knowing that grace is a core value in your home.

By taking these steps, you'll not only find peace in God's forgiveness, but you'll also build stronger relationships with your children, grounded in grace and understanding.

Closing Prayer

Heavenly Father, I come before You acknowledging my failures as a father. There have been times when I've fallen short, and the weight of those mistakes has been heavy on my heart. But I thank You for Your promise in Romans 8:1, that there is no condemnation for those who are in Christ Jesus. I ask for Your forgiveness and for the strength to forgive myself. Help me to move forward, trusting in Your grace and relying on Your strength. Lord, guide me to be the father my children need, not through my own perfection, but through Your love and wisdom. When I stumble, remind me to turn to You for renewal. Thank You for Your unending grace and for the assurance that I am not defined by my failures, but by Your love. In Jesus' name, Amen.

Week 12: Handling Stress in Fatherhood

"Do not be anxious about anything, but in every situation, by prayer and petition, with thanksgiving, present your requests to God. And the peace of God, which transcends all understanding, will guard your hearts and your minds in Christ Jesus."

(Philippians 4:6-7, NIV)

Daily Bible Reading

Sunday: Philippians 4:6-7   **Thursday**: Isaiah 40:31

Monday: Matthew 11:28-30   **Friday**: Psalm 34:17-19

Tuesday: Psalm 55:22   **Saturday**: Matthew 6:34

Wednesday: 1 Peter 5:7

Reflection

Fatherhood is full of responsibility. From providing financially to nurturing emotionally, the weight can often feel overwhelming. The stress of being a father is a unique burden because it affects every aspect of your life. You want to give your children the best, but at the same time, you're often juggling work, relationships, personal health, and spiritual growth. The pressure to be a good father can lead to feelings of inadequacy, exhaustion, and stress.

Philippians 4:6-7 provides a powerful antidote to the anxieties of fatherhood. It reminds us not to be anxious, but to bring everything to God in prayer. The reality of stress is inevitable, but how we handle it can make all the difference. God calls us to turn our stress into prayer, trusting that He will give us the peace we need to face our responsibilities.

As a father, you may feel like you must always be the strong one, the provider, the problem-solver. But God doesn't ask you to carry this burden alone. In fact, He invites you to cast your anxieties on Him. The stress of fatherhood might come from trying to control too many things at once—work pressures, financial difficulties, your children's future, or even personal doubts about your capabilities as a dad. It's easy to feel like the weight of the world rests on your shoulders, but it doesn't have to be that way.

Imagine a father struggling to balance work and family. He feels the pressure to succeed in his career so he can provide financially, but at the same time, he knows his children need his presence at home. The stress mounts as he realizes he can't be in two places at once. But rather than allowing this stress to consume him, he takes a moment to bring his concerns to God in prayer. He doesn't have the solution yet, but as he prays, he feels a sense of peace wash over him. God reminds him that it's okay to trust Him with both his job and his family.

That's the peace Philippians 4:6-7 talks about—the peace that surpasses understanding. It's the kind of peace that doesn't necessarily come from a change in circumstances, but from a change in perspective. When you bring your stress to God, He may not immediately remove the source of stress, but He promises to guard your heart and mind with peace. This peace allows you to face your responsibilities with a calm spirit, knowing that God is with you every step of the way.

One of the keys to managing stress in fatherhood is recognizing that you're not alone in this journey. God sees every burden you carry, and He wants you to trust Him with it. Instead of carrying the weight of fatherhood on your own, make a habit of handing over each concern to God in prayer. As you do, you'll find that His peace will sustain you, even when life feels overwhelming.

Another important aspect of managing stress is setting realistic expectations for yourself. You can't do everything perfectly, and that's okay. Your children don't need a perfect father — they need a loving and present one. By relying on God's grace and strength, you can show your children that even in times of stress, there is peace and hope to be found in Christ.

Action Step

Here are some practical steps to help you handle stress as a father:

1. **Identify and Pray About a Specific Source of Stress**: Take a few moments to reflect on what's been causing you the most stress lately. Is it work? Finances? Parenting challenges? Once you've identified the source, commit it to God in prayer. Ask Him to take control of the situation and to give you peace as you trust Him with the outcome.

2. **Set Boundaries to Manage Stress**: If possible, set some boundaries in your daily routine to protect yourself from becoming overwhelmed. This might mean limiting your work hours or scheduling regular breaks where you can relax and recharge. Prioritize family time without distractions, allowing yourself to be fully present with your children. When you manage your time and energy well, you'll find it easier to cope with stress.

3. **Engage in a Stress-Relief Activity with Your Family**: Sometimes, the best way to relieve stress is by spending quality time with your family. Choose an activity that allows you to bond with your children while also giving you a break from the pressures of life. Whether it's a simple walk in the park, playing a game, or sharing a meal together, these moments can help put things in perspective and remind you of the joy that comes from being a father.

By turning your stress over to God and taking practical steps to manage it, you'll be better equipped to lead your family with peace and confidence.

Closing Prayer

Heavenly Father, I come to You with the stresses and burdens of fatherhood weighing heavy on my heart. I know that You see every challenge I face, and I thank You for the promise of Your peace in Philippians 4:6-7. Help me to turn my stress into prayer and trust You with every detail of my life. Lord, I ask for Your peace to guard my heart and mind, especially in moments when I feel overwhelmed. Guide me to be the father my children need, not in my own strength, but through Your grace. Help me to set healthy boundaries, to be present with my family, and to rely on You in all things. Thank You for being my constant source of strength and for the peace that surpasses all understanding. In Jesus' name, Amen.

Week 13: Trusting God's Timing

"He has made everything beautiful in its time. He has also set eternity in the human heart; yet no one can fathom what God has done from beginning to end." (Ecclesiastes 3:11, NIV)

Daily Bible Reading

Sunday: Ecclesiastes 3:11

Monday: Isaiah 40:31

Tuesday: 2 Peter 3:9

Wednesday: Psalm 37:7

Thursday: Romans 8:28

Friday: Galatians 6:9

Saturday: James 5:7-8

Reflection

As fathers, we often desire to see immediate results in the lives of our children, especially in their spiritual growth. We want them to develop a strong relationship with God, to make wise decisions, and to live according to biblical principles. However, spiritual growth, much like physical growth, takes time. Impatience can easily set in when progress seems slow or when our children don't seem to be growing in their faith as quickly as we hoped. This can lead to frustration and even feelings of failure as a father.

Ecclesiastes 3:11 reminds us that God makes everything beautiful in His time. This verse is a powerful reminder that God's timing is perfect, even when we can't see the full picture. As fathers, it's important to trust that God is working in the hearts of our children, even when the results aren't immediately visible. Spiritual growth isn't something that can be rushed or forced. Just as a seed needs time to grow into a tree, our children's faith journey needs time to develop and mature.

Impatience can cause us to become overbearing, pushing our children too hard or expecting immediate change. But God calls us to trust Him with the process. It's not our job to control the timeline of their spiritual growth, but to guide them with love, patience, and consistency. Your role as a father is to plant seeds of faith, nurture them, and trust that God will bring the growth in His own time.

Consider the example of a father who has been praying for his child to develop a stronger prayer life. Week after week, he encourages his child to pray, but it seems like nothing is happening. Frustration builds as the father wonders if he's doing something wrong. But what he doesn't see is that, behind the scenes, God is working in his child's heart. Perhaps the child is thinking more deeply about faith, but it hasn't yet manifested in visible ways. In God's timing, those seeds will begin to grow, and the father will see the fruits of his patience and trust.

Trusting God's timing means releasing the desire for immediate results and believing that He is in control. God's plan for your children's lives is bigger than you can imagine, and it unfolds in His perfect timing. Your job is to remain faithful, to continue nurturing their spiritual growth, and to surrender your impatience to God. Let Him do the work that only He can do.

Remember, God is patient with all of us. He waits for us to grow and learn at our own pace, never rushing the process. As fathers, we can follow His example by exercising patience with our children. When we trust God's timing, we experience peace and relief from the pressure of trying to force results. We can rest in the assurance that He is working, even when we don't see it.

Action Step

Here are some practical steps to help you surrender impatience and trust God's timing in your children's spiritual growth:

1. **Surrender Your Impatience in Prayer**: Take a moment this week to pray specifically about any impatience you've been feeling regarding your children's spiritual growth. Bring your frustrations and concerns to God, and ask Him to give you the patience to wait on His timing. Trust that He is working in ways you may not see.

2. **Encourage Small Spiritual Habits**: Rather than focusing on big, immediate changes, encourage small, consistent spiritual habits in your family's daily life. This could be a short prayer before meals, a weekly Bible verse to memorize, or a quiet time to reflect on God's goodness. These small steps will add up over time and help build a foundation of faith in your children.

3. **Practice Patience in Conversations**: This week, have a gentle and patient conversation with your children about their faith. Instead of pushing for immediate results, ask open-ended questions like, "What has God been teaching you lately?" or "How do you feel about your relationship with God?" This will help you understand where they are in their journey and allow you to guide them without pressure.

By practicing these steps, you'll create an environment where your children feel supported in their spiritual growth, without the stress of meeting immediate expectations. Trust that God is at work, even when progress seems slow.

Closing Prayer

Heavenly Father, I come to You today, surrendering my impatience and frustrations over my children's spiritual growth. I know that Your timing is perfect, and I trust that You are working in their hearts, even when I don't see immediate results. Lord, help me to be a patient and loving father, guiding my children with wisdom and grace. Give me the strength to wait on Your timing and to trust in Your plan for their lives. Let me be a source of encouragement and support, never rushing their journey, but trusting that You are making everything beautiful in its time. Thank You for Your patience with me and for the work You are doing in my family. In Jesus' name, Amen.

Week 14: Being Present Amid Distractions

"Be still, and know that I am God; I will be exalted among the nations, I will be exalted in the earth." (Psalm 46:10, NIV)

Reflection

In today's fast-paced world, fathers often face the constant struggle of being pulled in many directions. Work demands, personal goals, social engagements, and even technology can steal time and attention away from what matters most—being present with your family. The pressure to succeed professionally or keep up with external distractions can leave little room for meaningful moments at home.

Psalm 46:10 calls us to "Be still, and know that I am God." This is a profound reminder that amidst the busyness of life, we are called to pause, reflect, and be present. Being present with your family doesn't simply mean being physically there, but being emotionally and mentally engaged. Your children need more than your presence—they need your attention, your listening ear, and your full heart.

Distractions can range from seemingly important tasks like work emails to the ever-present pull of social media or the constant buzzing of notifications. These distractions rob you of precious time with your family, and over time, they create distance in relationships. Children can sense when your mind is elsewhere, even when you're physically in the room. They need to feel that they are a priority in your life, not just another task on your to-do list.

Consider the story of a father who comes home from work but spends most of the evening on his phone or laptop. His children may be playing nearby, but they quickly learn that they have to compete with his devices for attention. Over time, this can create a disconnect, and the father might miss out on important moments in his children's lives. However, when the father makes a conscious effort to put down his phone and engage with his children—whether it's playing a game, having a conversation, or reading together—the family bond strengthens, and his presence becomes a gift to his children.

Being present requires intentionality. It means setting aside distractions and making time for what truly matters. Your work will always be there, but your children are only young once. The moments you spend with them now are priceless, and they form the foundation of a lasting relationship. When you choose to be fully present, you're teaching your children that they are valued and loved.

Action Step

This week, take practical steps to eliminate distractions and be more present with your family. Here's how you can start:

1. **Set Boundaries with Technology**: Make a commitment to limit the use of devices during family time. Create "no phone zones" during meals, bedtime routines, or family activities. This simple boundary will help you focus on meaningful interactions without the constant pull of notifications.

2. **Schedule Uninterrupted Family Time**: Set aside a specific time each day or week for uninterrupted family time. Whether it's a family dinner, game night, or outdoor activity, make this time non-negotiable. During this time, focus solely on being present with your family—ask questions, share stories, and listen actively.

3. **Practice Being Still**: Take a few moments each day to practice being still before God. Reflect on Psalm 46:10 and ask God to help you recognize areas of distraction in your life. Ask for guidance in being fully present with your family and in prioritizing what matters most.

These steps will help you create a more intentional family life, free from the distractions that often pull you away from meaningful connections. Your presence is a gift that will leave a lasting impact on your children.

Closing Prayer

Heavenly Father, I come to You today, asking for Your help in being fully present with my family. In a world filled with distractions, it's easy to lose focus on what truly matters. Lord, teach me to be still and know that You are God. Help me to set aside the distractions of work, technology, and the busyness of life, so that I can be fully engaged with my children and my spouse. Guide me to prioritize my family and to be a father who listens, loves, and invests in meaningful moments. Thank You for the gift of my family, and help me to cherish every moment with them. In Jesus' name, Amen.

Week 15: Overcoming Parental Guilt

"Therefore, there is now no condemnation for those who are in Christ Jesus." (Romans 8:1, NIV)

Daily Bible Reading

Sunday: Romans 8:1

Monday: Psalm 103:12

Tuesday: 1 John 1:9

Wednesday: Isaiah 43:25

Thursday: 2 Corinthians 5:17

Friday: Hebrews 8:12

Saturday: Micah 7:19

Reflection

Being a father is filled with moments of great joy, but it's also a journey of mistakes and imperfections. No matter how much you love your children or how hard you try, you've likely found yourself falling short at times. Perhaps you've spoken out of frustration, missed important moments, or made decisions that you now regret. These moments can leave you with lingering feelings of guilt, as though you've failed your children and yourself.

Parental guilt is something most fathers face at one point or another. It's that nagging voice in your head that says you're not doing enough or that your mistakes have caused irreversible damage. Left unchecked, this guilt can build over time, becoming a heavy burden that affects how you view yourself as a father. But Romans 8:1 offers an important truth: "Therefore, there is now no condemnation for those who are in Christ Jesus."

This verse is a powerful reminder that, while you may make mistakes, God does not condemn you for them. Through Christ, you are forgiven, and you are free from the weight of guilt and shame. God's grace covers your imperfections, and His love is greater than any mistake you've made as a father. Just as you extend grace and forgiveness to your children when they fall short, God extends the same grace to you.

It's essential to remember that no father is perfect. You're not expected to get everything right all the time. What matters is your heart—your desire to love, guide, and provide for your children. Mistakes are inevitable, but they are not the end of the story. God offers you the chance to learn, grow, and become a better father through His grace. Accepting God's forgiveness allows you to release the guilt and move forward with confidence in His love.

Imagine a father who regrets a harsh word spoken in anger. He feels the weight of that moment, worrying that his child's trust may be damaged. But instead of carrying that guilt, he chooses to seek God's forgiveness and goes to his child to apologize. Through this act of humility, the relationship is restored, and both the father and child learn the power of grace. This is what God invites you to do: acknowledge your mistakes, seek His forgiveness, and move forward in love.

God's grace isn't just a one-time offering—it's available every day, in every moment. When you feel overwhelmed by guilt, remind yourself of Romans 8:1. You are not condemned. You are a father who is loved, forgiven, and given the opportunity to start anew. By accepting this truth, you can let go of the past and focus on being the father God has called you to be.

Action Step

This week, take the following steps to release parental guilt and embrace God's grace in your role as a father:

1. **List One Past Mistake and Release It to God**: Reflect on a specific mistake you've been carrying as a father—whether it's something recent or a regret from years ago. Write it down and acknowledge it before God. Then, surrender it to Him in prayer, asking for His forgiveness and the strength to move

forward without guilt. This is a symbolic way of letting go and accepting God's grace.

2. **Have a Conversation with Your Child**: If your guilt is tied to a specific incident with your child, take time this week to have an open and honest conversation with them. Apologize if necessary and explain that, just like them, you're learning and growing as a father. This will not only restore the relationship but also teach your child about grace and forgiveness.

3. **Start a Family Prayer Time Focused on Grace**: Gather your family and have a prayer time dedicated to the theme of grace. Encourage everyone, including your children, to reflect on mistakes they've made and to ask for God's forgiveness. This will create a family culture of grace, where everyone understands that mistakes are opportunities to learn and grow.

By taking these steps, you'll begin to release the guilt that has weighed you down and embrace the freedom that comes from God's forgiveness. You'll also teach your children the powerful lesson that no one is perfect, but God's grace is always available.

Closing Prayer

Heavenly Father, I come before You today, acknowledging the guilt I've carried for the mistakes I've made as a father. I know I'm not perfect, but I thank You for Your grace that covers my imperfections. Lord, help me to release the burden of guilt and accept the forgiveness You offer so freely. Remind me that there is no condemnation for those who are in Christ Jesus, and help me to walk in the freedom of Your grace. Teach me to forgive myself and to grow from my mistakes, becoming the father You've called me to be. Lord, guide me in my relationships with my children, and help me to model grace, love, and humility in all that I do. Thank You for loving me and for the opportunity to start fresh each day. In Jesus' name, Amen.

Week 16: Encouraging Emotional Vulnerability as a Father

"The Lord is close to the brokenhearted and saves those who are crushed in spirit." (Psalm 34:18, NIV)

Daily Bible Reading

Sunday: Psalm 34:18

Monday: 2 Corinthians 12:9

Tuesday: Matthew 11:28-30

Wednesday: Psalm 147:3

Thursday: 1 Peter 5:7

Friday: Philippians 4:6-7

Saturday: Isaiah 41:10

Reflection

As fathers, society often places an expectation on us to always be strong, resilient, and composed. We believe that showing any form of emotional vulnerability could be seen as a sign of weakness. However, God never intended for fathers to carry the weight of emotional struggles alone or to suppress their feelings. Rather, He calls us to be authentic, especially within our families, and to lean on His strength in our moments of weakness.

Psalm 34:18 speaks directly to this: "The Lord is close to the brokenhearted and saves those who are crushed in spirit." This verse offers a comforting reminder that God draws near when we are struggling, not when we are pretending to have everything under control. He doesn't expect us to bottle up our emotions. Instead, He invites us to bring them to Him, knowing that He is compassionate and close to those who are hurting.

Many fathers grapple with the pressure of appearing invincible in front of their children, spouses, and peers. This expectation can lead to a deep sense of isolation, as we try to manage our frustrations, fears, or disappointments on our own. But when we model emotional vulnerability, we teach our children that it's okay to feel, to express their emotions, and to lean on God during difficult times. Vulnerability doesn't make us weaker as fathers; it makes us more authentic, approachable, and grounded in God's grace.

Imagine a father who has been struggling with the stress of work and financial pressures. He feels overwhelmed, yet every day he puts on a brave face for his family. One evening, he sits down with his wife and children, and instead of hiding his feelings, he opens up about the stress he's been experiencing. He shares how he's been praying for strength and guidance, but he also admits that he needs their support and prayers. This simple act of vulnerability not only strengthens the bond within the family but also shows his children that it's okay to acknowledge their emotions and seek help.

As fathers, when we allow ourselves to be vulnerable, we create a safe space for our families to be open about their own feelings. We demonstrate that our strength doesn't come from pretending we have everything under control but from relying on God's grace and wisdom. Vulnerability is a gift, not a flaw—it opens the door to deeper relationships with both our families and our Heavenly Father.

God doesn't expect you to carry your emotional burdens alone. He promises to be near when you are brokenhearted and crushed in spirit. When you embrace this truth, you can let go of the unrealistic expectation of always being strong and trust that God's strength is made perfect in your weakness. This week, challenge yourself to be more emotionally transparent with your family. By doing so, you'll model an important truth for your children: that real strength comes from depending on God and allowing others to walk with you through life's challenges.

Action Step

Here are a few practical steps to help you embrace emotional vulnerability as a father:

1. **Have a Vulnerable Conversation with Your Family**: Set aside time this week to have an honest conversation with your spouse and children about something you've been struggling with emotionally. This could be stress from work, anxiety about finances, or even feelings of fear or failure. Use this opportunity to show your family that it's okay to express emotions and ask for support.
2. **Pray Over Your Emotional Burdens**: Each day this week, spend time in prayer, asking God to help you release the emotional burdens you've been carrying. Be specific about the areas where you've been struggling and ask God to fill those spaces with His peace and strength. Trust that He is near to you in these moments, just as Psalm 34:18 promises.
3. **Create an Emotionally Safe Space for Your Children**: Make a conscious effort to encourage emotional openness in your home. Ask your children how they're feeling and listen without judgment. Share a story of your own emotional journey, and remind them that God is always there to comfort and strengthen them, just as He is for you.

By taking these steps, you'll foster an atmosphere of emotional honesty in your home, where every family member feels safe to share their burdens and experience God's grace in their vulnerability.

Closing Prayer

Heavenly Father, I come to You today with the emotional burdens I've been carrying. I admit that I often try to hide my struggles, believing that I must always be strong. But Your Word reminds me that You are close to the brokenhearted and that I don't have to carry these burdens alone. Lord, help me to embrace emotional vulnerability, not as a weakness, but as an opportunity to trust in Your strength. Give me the courage to open up to my family and to lean on their support, knowing that together we can rely on You. Teach me to model honesty and authenticity for my children, showing them that it's okay to feel deeply and to bring our emotions to You in prayer. Thank You for being my comfort and my strength, especially in my moments of weakness. In Jesus' name, I pray. Amen.

Week 17: Managing Anger as a Dad

"A gentle answer turns away wrath, but a harsh word stirs up anger." (Proverbs 15:1, NIV)

Reflection

Anger is an emotion that every father deals with at some point, especially when faced with the daily challenges of raising children. Whether it's the frustration that arises from disobedience, the stress of balancing responsibilities, or the weariness that sets in after a long day, anger can quickly take root if not handled carefully. Many fathers struggle with the feeling that they need to be in control, and when things don't go as planned, anger becomes a natural reaction.

Proverbs 15:1 provides a wise counsel: "A gentle answer turns away wrath, but a harsh word stirs up anger." This verse reminds us that the way we respond to our children—and to any situation—can either diffuse or escalate tension. When we speak gently and calmly, we create an atmosphere of peace, but when we let anger take control, it often leads to harsh words, which can damage relationships, especially with our children.

As a father, managing anger is not just about avoiding outbursts; it's about understanding the root of that anger and turning to God for help. Frustration often stems from unmet expectations, exhaustion, or feeling overwhelmed by the many responsibilities that come with fatherhood. But instead of allowing these feelings to fester and explode, God invites us to bring them to Him in prayer.

Real-life examples abound. Think of a time when your child repeatedly ignored your instructions or when a chaotic morning left you running late for work. It's easy for anger to build up, but reacting in frustration may lead to words or actions that cause hurt. Later, you may regret the way you handled the situation. This is the cycle many fathers experience—anger followed by guilt.

However, there is hope. Managing anger as a dad doesn't mean you will never feel frustrated again; it means learning to pause, reflect, and turn to God in those heated moments. The power of prayer and the guidance of the Holy Spirit can help you develop patience and self-control, even when parenting feels overwhelming.

One way to do this is by identifying your anger triggers. Perhaps it's the stress of work or the noise and chaos at home. When you recognize what fuels your frustration, you can prepare yourself spiritually and emotionally to respond with patience and calmness. This doesn't mean suppressing your feelings—it means processing them in a healthy way. Instead of snapping at your child, take a moment to breathe, ask for God's guidance, and remember that your reaction shapes how your child learns to deal with their own emotions.

Anger management as a father is a journey. There will be moments of failure, but by turning to God, you can learn from those moments and grow. Proverbs 15:1 is not just about avoiding conflict but about building an environment in your home where grace and understanding rule, even in difficult situations.

Action Step

Here are a few practical steps to help you manage anger and frustration as a father:

1. **Identify Your Trigger Points**: Take time this week to reflect on what triggers your anger. Is it specific behaviors from your children? The stress of work? Lack of rest? Once you identify these triggers, you can prepare yourself to handle them calmly. Write them down and pray over them, asking God to give you peace in those moments.

2. **Practice Pausing Before Responding**: In moments of frustration, commit to pausing before you react. Take a deep breath, count to five, or say a quick prayer asking God for patience. This simple act of pausing can help prevent harsh words and give you time to respond with gentleness.

3. **Use Scripture to Guide Your Response**: Memorize Proverbs 15:1 this week and meditate on it whenever you feel anger rising. Let the words of Scripture remind you of the power of a gentle answer. Before addressing your child's behavior or responding to a situation, ask yourself, "How can I answer gently in this moment?"

By implementing these steps, you'll not only manage your anger better but also model for your children how to handle frustration in a Christ-like way. The goal is not perfection but progress, and with God's help, you can respond to challenges with calmness and grace.

Closing Prayer

Heavenly Father, I come to You today, acknowledging the struggle I have with anger and frustration as a father. Lord, I ask for Your help in managing my emotions and responding with gentleness, even in the most difficult moments. Your Word tells me that a gentle answer turns away wrath, but I know that I cannot do this on my own. I need Your strength and Your peace to guide my words and actions.

Help me to recognize the triggers that lead to anger, and give me the wisdom to pause and seek Your guidance before I respond. Teach me to be patient with my children and to lead them with love, even when I feel overwhelmed. Thank You for being close to me in my struggles and for offering me the grace to grow as a father. In Jesus' name, I pray. Amen.

Week 18: Teaching Your Children About God's Love

"These commandments that I give you today are to be on your hearts. Impress them on your children. Talk about them when you sit at home and when you walk along the road, when you lie down and when you get up." (Deuteronomy 6:6-7, NIV)

Daily Bible Reading

Sunday: Deuteronomy 6:6-7

Monday: Proverbs 22:6

Tuesday: Ephesians 6:4

Wednesday: Psalm 78:4

Thursday: 2 Timothy 3:14-15

Friday: Matthew 19:14

Saturday: 1 John 4:19

Reflection

As fathers, one of the most important responsibilities we have is to teach our children about God's love. Yet, many of us struggle with feelings of inadequacy when it comes to being a spiritual leader in the home. We may feel that we don't have enough biblical knowledge or worry that we might not live up to the example of faith we hope to set. But God calls us not to perfection, but to faithfulness. Deuteronomy 6:6-7 reminds us that teaching our children about God isn't something reserved for grand moments, but a daily practice that happens in the rhythm of everyday life.

This scripture emphasizes the importance of integrating faith into all aspects of life—whether at home, on the road, or during the simple moments of the day. Teaching our children about God's love doesn't have to be a formal sermon or a polished Bible study. It's the consistent example of living out faith that speaks the loudest. Whether it's praying before meals, reading a short Bible story before bed, or taking a few minutes to share how God has worked in your life, these simple acts of devotion leave a lasting impact on your children's hearts.

Feeling inadequate is a common experience among fathers, especially in matters of faith. But remember that God has already equipped you for this task. You don't need to have all the answers or be a perfect role model—God's grace is sufficient, and His Word is your guide. What your children need most is to see a father who seeks God, who admits when he falls short, and who relies on God's strength.

One of the most powerful ways to teach your children about God's love is through your own actions. They will watch how you handle stress, how you respond to challenges, and how you treat others. Your example of love, patience, and humility speaks louder than any words you can say. You can also teach through intentional conversations—sharing personal stories of faith or explaining how God's love has shaped your own journey. These moments of vulnerability show your children that faith is not just a concept, but a lived reality.

It's important to remember that teaching your children about faith is not a one-time event, but a lifelong journey. You won't get it right every time, and that's okay. Just as you are learning and growing in your faith, so too are your children. The key is to be intentional and consistent, trusting that God will work through your efforts, no matter how small they seem. Over time, these seeds of faith will take root and grow in your children's hearts.

Action Step

Here are some practical steps you can take this week to teach your children about God's love:

1. **Share a Bible Story**: Choose a simple Bible story that illustrates God's love (such as the parable of the Prodigal Son or Jesus feeding the 5,000) and share it with your children this

week. After reading the story, ask them what they learned about God's love and take time to explain how it applies to their lives.

2. **Create Daily Faith Moments**: Incorporate faith into the everyday moments of life. Whether it's praying together before bed or having a short conversation about what you're thankful for at the dinner table, use these moments to reinforce God's presence in your family's life. It doesn't have to be elaborate; consistency is more important than complexity.

3. **Live Out God's Love**: Show your children what God's love looks like in action. Find a way to serve others as a family this week, whether through acts of kindness, helping a neighbor, or supporting someone in need. These tangible expressions of love will help your children see how faith leads to action.

By taking these steps, you will not only teach your children about God's love through words but also through actions and daily habits. Remember, it's not about being perfect, but about being faithful in the small moments.

Closing Prayer

Heavenly Father, I thank You for the gift of being a father and for the opportunity to teach my children about Your love. I confess that at times I feel inadequate in this role, but I trust that You are with me, guiding my steps. Help me to be a faithful example of Your love, both in my words and actions. Give me wisdom as I lead my children in faith and courage to admit when I fall short. Lord, help me to integrate faith into the everyday moments of life so that my children will see You in everything we do. Open their hearts to know You more deeply and to understand the depth of Your love for them. I commit this task to You, trusting that You will work through me to shape their hearts and guide them on their own spiritual journeys. In Jesus' name, I pray. Amen.

Week 19: Facing Personal Doubts as a Father

"But when you ask, you must believe and not doubt, because the one who doubts is like a wave of the sea, blown and tossed by the wind." (James 1:6, NIV)

Daily Bible Reading

Sunday: James 1:6

Monday: Proverbs 3:5-6

Tuesday: Psalm 25:4-5

Wednesday: Isaiah 40:29-31

Thursday: Philippians 4:13

Friday: 2 Corinthians 12:9-10

Saturday: Romans 8:28

Reflection

As a father, it's natural to face moments of doubt. Whether it's questioning your ability to raise your children in faith, worrying about providing for your family, or simply wondering if you're enough, these doubts can creep in and weigh heavily on your heart. You might find yourself thinking, "Am I really capable of being the father my children need?" These feelings are common, but the good news is that God equips you for this vital role.

James 1:6 encourages us to ask God for wisdom but to do so in faith, without doubt. When we approach God with our uncertainties, we must believe that He will provide the guidance and strength we need. Doubts can feel overwhelming, but they are often an opportunity to deepen our reliance on God. Rather than viewing your doubts as failures, see them as invitations to trust in God's provision and His plan for you as a father.

One of the most significant challenges fathers face is the weight of responsibility. It can be daunting to realize that your words and actions shape your children's understanding of love, faith, and life. This pressure can lead to self-doubt, especially when you fall short or make mistakes. But remember, God doesn't expect perfection—He calls for faithfulness. He knows your weaknesses, and He is ready to fill the gaps with His grace.

Consider a father who feels inadequate in guiding his children spiritually. He may not have all the answers, and sometimes he might worry that his efforts won't bear fruit. However, this is where faith comes into play. God calls you to plant seeds, to be present, and to trust that He will bring growth in His own time. It's not your job to have everything figured out; your role is to lead with love and point your children toward God's truth.

Fathers often carry hidden fears—fears of not being able to provide, of failing to protect, or of making irreversible mistakes. These fears can lead to feelings of inadequacy and doubt. Yet, God promises in His Word that when we feel weak, He is strong (2 Corinthians 12:9). This means that even in your moments of doubt, God's grace is sufficient. He knows what you need as a father, and He is faithful to equip you for every situation you face.

Trusting God to equip you as a father doesn't mean the journey will be easy. You will have moments of failure and doubt. But it's in these moments that God asks you to lean on Him more deeply. He invites you to bring your doubts and fears to Him, knowing that He has already prepared you for the role He has called you to.

Doubt can be a heavy burden, but it's also a reminder to stay anchored in God's promises. When you place your trust in Him, He turns your doubts into opportunities for growth. As you face your doubts, remember that God sees your heart. He knows the love you have for your children, and He is faithful to guide you, even when you feel unsure.

Action Step

Here are a few practical steps to help you overcome personal doubts and grow in confidence as a father:

1. **Pray for Wisdom and Trust God's Guidance**: This week, make a point to pray specifically for wisdom in the areas where you feel unsure as a father. Ask God to reveal His guidance to you, and trust that He will equip you with what you need. Remember James 1:6—when you pray, do so with faith that God will answer.

2. **Acknowledge Your Strengths**: Reflect on the positive ways you've impacted your children's lives. Write down one or two specific examples of moments where you felt like you made a positive difference as a father. This practice can help counterbalance doubt and remind you of God's work through you.

3. **Be Vulnerable with Your Family**: Share your doubts and concerns with your spouse or a trusted friend. Vulnerability creates space for support and encouragement. You don't have to carry your doubts alone—God often works through the people around you to provide reassurance and wisdom.

By taking these steps, you'll find that God is faithful in easing your doubts and replacing them with confidence. Trusting Him will strengthen not only your role as a father but also your walk of faith.

Closing Prayer

Heavenly Father, I come before You today with the doubts and fears I have as a father. At times, I feel overwhelmed and unsure of my ability to be the father my children need. But I know that You have called me to this role, and I trust that You will equip me with everything necessary to fulfill it. Lord, I ask for Your wisdom and guidance in the areas where I feel uncertain. Help me to trust in Your strength rather than my own. Remind me that I don't have to be perfect, but I do need to be faithful. Help me to lead my children with love, grace, and patience, relying on You every step of the way. I surrender my doubts to You, trusting that You will replace them with confidence in Your plan. Thank You for walking with me through this journey of fatherhood. In Jesus' name, I pray. Amen.

Week 20: Teaching Responsibility

"Whoever can be trusted with very little can also be trusted with much, and whoever is dishonest with very little will also be dishonest with much." (Luke 16:10, NIV)

Daily Bible Reading

Sunday: Luke 16:10

Monday: Proverbs 22:6

Tuesday: Colossians 3:23

Wednesday: Galatians 6:4-5

Thursday: Matthew 25:21

Friday: 1 Timothy 4:12

Saturday: Proverbs 12:24

Reflection

In today's world, the challenge of teaching children responsibility has never been greater. Everywhere they look, children are bombarded with messages of instant gratification—from quick online deliveries to immediate entertainment on digital platforms. The idea that hard work, persistence, and discipline pay off over time can often be overshadowed by a world that promises quick fixes and shortcuts. As fathers, it's crucial to instill the value of responsibility in our children, helping them understand that life's rewards often come through consistent effort and faithfulness in the small things.

Luke 16:10 gives us an important principle: "Whoever can be trusted with very little can also be trusted with much." This verse highlights the importance of taking care of the small tasks, as they prepare us for greater responsibilities. Teaching children responsibility isn't just about getting them to do their chores—it's about shaping their character and preparing them for the future. When they learn to be responsible in the little things, they're also learning how to handle bigger challenges down the road, whether in school, work, or relationships.

One of the greatest obstacles in teaching responsibility is the temptation to rescue our children from their mistakes. It's hard to watch them struggle, fail, or take longer than we'd like to complete a task. But by stepping in too quickly, we may unintentionally rob them of the lessons they need to learn. Responsibility is built when children are allowed to experience the consequences of their actions—both good and bad. When they see that their efforts lead to positive outcomes, they grow in confidence. When they experience the negative consequences of neglecting their duties, they learn the value of diligence.

As fathers, it's easy to take on too much for our children, whether because we feel we can do it faster or better. But our role is to guide them, not do everything for them. By assigning age-appropriate tasks and holding our children accountable, we are teaching them life skills that will serve them for years to come. Responsibility also builds trust between father and child. When a child sees that their father trusts them with a task, it instills a sense of pride and ownership in their work. They learn that they are capable and that their contributions matter.

It's important to remember that teaching responsibility doesn't happen overnight. It requires patience and persistence. Children will make mistakes along the way, but these are opportunities for growth. Use these moments to encourage them rather than criticize. Help them see that responsibility is not about being perfect—it's about being faithful in their efforts and learning from their missteps.

Just as God entrusts us with responsibilities in our lives, we are called to teach our children the same principle. It's through the small, consistent actions of responsibility that our character is formed, and the same is true for our children. By guiding them in this, we are helping them become people who can be trusted with more in the future.

Action Step

Here are a few practical steps to teach responsibility to your children this week:

1. **Assign a New Responsibility**: This week, choose a new responsibility for each of your children based on their age and abilities. Whether it's helping with household chores, managing their schoolwork independently, or caring for a pet, make sure the task is clear and manageable. Explain the importance of this responsibility and how it helps the family or community.

2. **Hold Them Accountable**: Once the task has been assigned, follow through with regular check-ins. Ask your child how they are handling the responsibility, but avoid stepping in to do the task for them. Offer encouragement, but also allow them to experience the natural consequences if they neglect their duties. This teaches them that their actions have results—whether positive or negative.

3. **Celebrate Effort, Not Perfection**: Focus on celebrating the effort your children put into their responsibilities rather than expecting perfection. If they've done their best, acknowledge their hard work and how it contributes to the family. This encourages them to continue being responsible and builds their confidence in handling bigger tasks in the future.

By taking these steps, you will help your children understand that responsibility is an essential part of life and that it's something to be embraced, not avoided. Over time, they will see the rewards of their efforts and begin to take pride in their contributions to the family and community.

Closing Prayer

Heavenly Father, thank You for the responsibility You've entrusted to me as a father. I know that teaching my children about responsibility is an important part of shaping their character, and I ask for Your guidance as I lead them in this. Help me to be patient when they struggle and to offer them grace as they learn. Give me wisdom in assigning tasks that will challenge them, but also give them the confidence to succeed. Lord, help me to model responsibility in my own life so that they can see Your principles at work through me. I pray that my children will grow to understand the value of being faithful in the small things, knowing that You will entrust them with more as they prove themselves trustworthy. Thank You for walking with me through this journey of fatherhood. In Jesus' name, I pray. Amen.

Week 21: Coping with Exhaustion

"But those who hope in the Lord will renew their strength. They will soar on wings like eagles; they will run and not grow weary, they will walk and not be faint." (Isaiah 40:31, NIV)

Daily Bible Reading

Sunday: Isaiah 40:31

Monday: Matthew 11:28-30

Tuesday: Psalm 23:1-3

Wednesday: Philippians 4:13

Thursday: Psalm 46:10

Friday: Exodus 33:14

Saturday: 2 Corinthians 12:9

Reflection

Fatherhood is one of the greatest gifts, but it can also be exhausting. The daily tasks of providing for your family, guiding your children, and being present as a husband and father can take a toll on your physical, emotional, and spiritual well-being. Exhaustion often creeps in slowly, until one day you wake up feeling drained and wondering how you'll make it through the day. The demands of work, home, and relationships can pile up, leaving you feeling like there's nothing left to give.

Isaiah 40:31 offers a profound promise: those who hope in the Lord will renew their strength. This doesn't mean you'll never feel tired or overwhelmed—it means that in those moments when you feel like you've reached your limit, God offers to replenish your energy. He invites you to lean on Him for rest and renewal, allowing His strength to carry you through the most exhausting seasons of life.

As a father, it's easy to fall into the trap of trying to do everything on your own. You might feel like you have to be the provider, protector, and leader, all while hiding your own weariness. But

God doesn't expect you to carry the weight of fatherhood by yourself. He wants to partner with you, offering His strength in exchange for your burdens. When you surrender your exhaustion to Him, you're not admitting defeat—you're recognizing that you were never meant to carry it all alone.

Consider a father who works long hours to provide for his family, only to come home to the demands of household responsibilities and the emotional needs of his children. He feels pulled in every direction and wonders how he can continue to pour into his family when he feels so depleted. This father may try to push through, thinking that rest is a luxury he can't afford. Yet, this is precisely when God calls him to pause, rest, and receive the strength that only comes from God.

In moments of exhaustion, it's crucial to recognize the importance of rest—not just physical rest, but spiritual rest. God's Word reminds us that true rest is found in His presence. Psalm 23:1-3 speaks of God leading us beside quiet waters and restoring our soul. This kind of rest isn't just about taking a nap (though naps can be helpful!); it's about finding peace in God's presence, where He replenishes not just our bodies but our hearts and minds as well.

It's important to remember that exhaustion doesn't make you weak—it makes you human. Even Jesus, during His time on earth, took moments to withdraw and rest (Mark 6:31). He modeled for us the importance of stepping away from the demands of life to be renewed by God. As fathers, we need to follow His example. Taking time to rest in God's presence not only benefits you, but it also strengthens your ability to lead and love your family well.

When you feel overwhelmed, take comfort in the fact that God knows your limits. He doesn't ask you to push through on your own strength. Instead, He offers His own strength to help you carry the load. Isaiah 40:31 reminds us that when we put our hope in the Lord, we will soar on wings like eagles, run without growing weary, and walk without fainting. This is the promise you can hold onto in moments of exhaustion.

Action Step

Here are a few practical steps to help you cope with exhaustion as a father this week:

1. **Take Time to Rest in God's Presence**: This week, set aside time each day to rest in God's presence, even if it's just for a few minutes. Find a quiet place where you can sit and reflect on Scripture, pray, and allow God to renew your strength. You don't have to fill this time with words—simply being still before God and acknowledging your need for His help can bring peace and refreshment.
2. **Delegate and Share Responsibilities**: If you're feeling overwhelmed, take a look at your daily tasks and see where you can delegate or share responsibilities. Whether it's asking your spouse for help with household chores or teaching your children to take on more age-appropriate tasks, remember that you don't have to do everything on your own. Sharing the load is not a sign of weakness, but a sign of wisdom.
3. **Prioritize Rest**: Make rest a priority this week. It can be tempting to power through exhaustion, but rest is essential for your well-being and your ability to be present for your family. Whether it's going to bed earlier, taking a short walk during the day, or scheduling a quiet evening without distractions, find ways to physically and mentally rest.

By taking these steps, you'll not only address your exhaustion but also model for your children the importance of rest and reliance on God. They need to see that even their strong and capable father knows when to lean on God's strength.

Closing Prayer

Dear Heavenly Father, I come to You today feeling weary and worn. The demands of fatherhood are great, and at times, I feel like I have nothing left to give. But I know that in You, I can find rest and renewal. Thank You for the promise in Isaiah 40:31 that those who hope in You will renew their strength. I ask that You help me find peace in Your presence this week. Teach me to lean on You and not my own strength. Show me when to rest, when to ask for help, and when to release the burdens I've been carrying. Lord, I pray that You refresh my spirit so I can continue to lead and love my family well. Thank You for being my source of strength, even when I feel weak. I trust You to guide me through the moments of exhaustion and bring me to a place of peace and rest. In Jesus' name, I pray. Amen.

Week 22: Navigating Conflict in the Family

"Blessed are the peacemakers, for they will be called children of God." (Matthew 5:9, NIV)

Daily Bible Reading

Sunday: Matthew 5:9

Monday: Romans 12:18

Tuesday: Ephesians 4:2-3

Wednesday: Colossians 3:13

Thursday: Proverbs 15:1

Friday: James 1:19-20

Saturday: 1 Peter 3:9

Reflection

Family life is filled with moments of joy, love, and togetherness. However, it's also inevitable that conflict will arise, whether between siblings, parents, or the entire family. As a father, you often find yourself caught in the middle of these disputes, wondering how to best mediate while keeping the peace. Conflict can stem from small misunderstandings or escalate into larger issues that can strain family relationships. This is where your role as a father becomes vital. God has called you to be a peacemaker in your home.

Matthew 5:9 highlights the importance of being a peacemaker: "Blessed are the peacemakers, for they will be called children of God." This verse reminds us that being a peacemaker is not just about avoiding conflict but actively seeking to bring peace in moments of tension. It's about calming storms before they turn into destructive waves. As fathers, it can be tempting to either ignore conflict, hoping it will resolve itself, or to step in with authority and impose a quick fix. However, the heart of peacemaking is much more about wisdom, grace, and seeking unity than it is about control.

Conflict, while difficult, can also be an opportunity for growth. It's in these moments that your children learn how to navigate disagreements with love, patience, and understanding. However, if conflict is handled poorly—whether through harsh words, neglect, or anger—these moments can also tear at the very fabric of family unity. As fathers, we need to model how to handle conflict in a way that honors God and brings peace, even in the most challenging moments.

Consider a common scenario: a disagreement between siblings over who gets to play with a toy or use a shared device. As a father, your instinct might be to step in and immediately solve the issue by taking away the object in dispute. However, what if instead of just solving the problem for them, you use this as a teachable moment? You can encourage your children to express their feelings calmly, listen to one another, and find a resolution that honors both sides. In doing so, you are teaching them valuable skills they will use throughout their lives—not only in family matters but in friendships, school, and future work environments.

Of course, conflict isn't limited to children. Disagreements can also arise between you and your spouse. These conflicts are particularly important to navigate with care, as they set the tone for how your children view relationships and conflict resolution. If your children see you model humility, love, and patience in resolving disagreements, they will be more likely to adopt these qualities themselves.

It's also important to recognize that managing conflict doesn't mean avoiding it altogether. Conflict can lead to stronger relationships if handled with grace. Your role as a father is to create a safe space where feelings can be expressed openly and where resolution can be sought with kindness and understanding. This is especially true when the conflicts are about deeper issues—values, respect, or emotional needs.

As you step into this role of peacemaker, it's vital to rely on God's wisdom. You may not always have the perfect solution, but God promises to provide the grace you need to navigate these moments. James 1:19-20 reminds us to "be quick to listen, slow to speak, and slow to become angry." In the heat of conflict, it's often our first reaction to speak out of frustration or impatience. However, by pausing and asking God for wisdom, we can offer a calming presence that leads to peace rather than further division.

Action Step

Here are a few practical steps to help you navigate conflict in your family this week:

1. **Encourage Open Communication**: This week, create a safe space for family members to express their feelings without fear of judgment or immediate correction. Whether it's a sibling disagreement or a misunderstanding between you and your spouse, encourage everyone to share their thoughts calmly. Practice listening without interrupting and model this behavior for your children. Let them see that resolving conflict begins with truly hearing one another.
2. **Mediate with Grace and Wisdom**: When a conflict arises, instead of immediately solving it for your children or spouse, guide them through the process of reconciliation. Ask questions like, "How do you feel?" and "What do you think a fair solution might be?" Helping them navigate the conflict teaches problem-solving skills and fosters mutual respect. Be patient as they learn this skill—it takes time.

3. **Pray for Unity**: Conflict is inevitable, but division doesn't have to be. This week, make it a point to pray for unity in your family. Ask God to give you the wisdom to lead with grace and humility. In moments of tension, take a step back and ask for His guidance before responding. When you lead your family in prayer, you demonstrate that you are relying on God's wisdom, not just your own.

By taking these steps, you will help your family navigate conflicts in a way that strengthens relationships and brings peace into the home. Your role as a father isn't just to manage the conflict, but to guide your family through it with love, grace, and wisdom.

Closing Prayer

Heavenly Father, thank You for Your peace that surpasses all understanding. I ask for Your guidance as I navigate the conflicts that arise within my family. Help me to be a peacemaker, leading with wisdom, patience, and grace. When tempers flare or misunderstandings happen, give me the strength to remain calm and to listen with an open heart. Teach me to model the kind of love and understanding that reflects Your heart for unity. I pray that my family will learn to handle conflict in a way that honors You and brings us closer together. Lord, help me to rely on Your strength and wisdom, trusting that You are with me in every situation. Thank You for the gift of my family and the opportunity to grow together, even through difficult moments. In Jesus' name, I pray. Amen.

Week 23: Balancing Discipline with Compassion

"Fathers, do not embitter your children, or they will become discouraged." (Colossians 3:21, NIV)

Daily Bible Reading

Sunday: Colossians 3:21

Monday: Proverbs 13:24

Tuesday: Ephesians 6:4

Wednesday: James 1:19-20

Thursday: Matthew 7:12

Friday: Hebrews 12:6

Saturday: Proverbs 19:18

Reflection

One of the greatest challenges for fathers is finding the right balance between discipline and compassion. As fathers, we are responsible for guiding our children in the right direction, correcting them when necessary, and teaching them the values they need to grow into responsible, God-fearing adults. However, discipline that is too harsh or unkind can damage the relationship with our children and even cause them to become discouraged, as the Apostle Paul warns in Colossians 3:21.

It's easy to fall into the trap of reacting in the heat of the moment. Perhaps your child disobeyed a rule, and your first instinct is to issue a harsh punishment to assert authority. But as Christian fathers, we are called to a higher standard—discipline should always be tempered with love, grace, and understanding. God disciplines us as His children, but His correction is always wrapped in love. Hebrews 12:6 tells us that "the Lord disciplines the one he loves." This is the model we must follow with our children.

Balancing discipline with compassion doesn't mean being permissive or avoiding correction. Instead, it means delivering discipline in a way that shows our children that we love them, even in their mistakes. When we discipline without compassion, we risk embittering our children, making them feel unloved or resentful. But when we discipline with love, we help them understand that the correction is for their growth and well-being.

Consider the example of a child who has repeatedly ignored instructions about doing their chores. The frustration you feel as a father is understandable. However, instead of reacting with anger, a compassionate approach might involve sitting down with your child, explaining why their behavior is not acceptable, and discussing the importance of responsibility. You can then administer a consequence that is firm but loving—perhaps reducing their screen time until they complete their chores. This approach teaches responsibility without damaging the relationship or leaving your child feeling disheartened.

Compassion in discipline also requires us to listen. Sometimes, there are underlying issues behind disobedience or defiance. By taking the time to listen, we might discover that our child is struggling with something else—a problem at school, anxiety, or simply a desire for attention. Addressing these issues with understanding allows us to discipline in a way that builds up our children rather than tearing them down.

As fathers, we must also model self-control and patience. James 1:19 instructs us to be "quick to listen, slow to speak, and slow to become angry." When we lose our temper, we risk losing our children's trust. If we react out of anger, the discipline we give may cause more harm than good. On the other hand, if we approach correction with a calm and loving demeanor, we show our children that discipline is not about punishment, but about growth and learning.

Balancing discipline with compassion also involves teaching our children about grace. Just as we receive grace from God for our mistakes, we must offer grace to our children. This doesn't mean excusing bad behavior but rather providing an opportunity for redemption. When we correct our children, we can remind them that they have the chance to learn from their mistakes and do better next time.

In summary, discipline is a crucial aspect of fatherhood, but it must always be administered with compassion. Our goal is to guide our children toward maturity and responsibility while ensuring that they feel loved, supported, and understood. When we balance discipline with compassion, we reflect the heart of our heavenly Father, who disciplines us out of His great love for us.

Action Step

Here are a few practical steps to help you balance discipline with compassion this week:

1. **Pause Before Reacting**: The next time your child disobeys or acts out, take a moment to pause before responding. Use this time to pray for wisdom and calmness. This pause will help you avoid reacting in anger and allow you to approach the situation with a clear mind and compassionate heart.
2. **Listen First**: Before issuing discipline, take the time to listen to your child's side of the story. Ask questions and try to understand the root cause of their behavior. By showing that you are willing to listen, you foster a sense of trust and open communication.
3. **Explain the "Why" Behind the Discipline**: When correcting your child, explain why their behavior is unacceptable and what the consequences are. Use this as a teaching moment

rather than simply punishing them. Helping them understand the "why" helps them grow and learn from their mistakes.

4. **Follow Discipline with Love**: After you have disciplined your child, be sure to show them love and grace. Reassure them that they are still loved and valued, even when they make mistakes. A hug, kind words, or spending time together afterward can go a long way in maintaining a strong bond.

These steps will help you cultivate a balanced approach to discipline that corrects behavior while strengthening your relationship with your child.

Closing Prayer

Dear Heavenly Father, Thank You for Your example of love and discipline. I pray for Your wisdom as I guide my children. Help me to balance discipline with compassion, correcting them in a way that teaches and uplifts rather than discourages. Give me patience and self-control when I feel frustrated, and remind me to listen to their hearts. Lord, I ask for Your grace in moments of correction, that I may reflect Your love to my children. Let my discipline guide them toward responsibility, while my compassion reassures them of my unconditional love. Strengthen me to lead with gentleness, just as You lead me with love and kindness. In Jesus' name, I pray. Amen.

Week 24: Cultivating Gratitude in Your Children

"Give thanks in all circumstances; for this is God's will for you in Christ Jesus." (1 Thessalonians 5:18, NIV)

Daily Bible Reading

Sunday: 1 Thessalonians 5:18

Monday: Colossians 3:15

Tuesday: Psalm 100:4

Wednesday: Philippians 4:6

Thursday: James 1:17

Friday: Luke 17:15-16

Saturday: Psalm 136:1

Reflection

Raising children in a world that constantly promotes materialism and the pursuit of more can be one of the most significant challenges for Christian fathers. Our culture often values possessions, achievements, and status over contentment, and this can make it difficult to teach our children the importance of gratitude. As fathers, we want our children to understand that true joy and contentment come not from having more but from recognizing and appreciating the blessings we already have.

1 Thessalonians 5:18 reminds us to "give thanks in all circumstances," which encourages us to model gratitude not just during good times but also when life presents challenges. Teaching children to be thankful goes beyond instructing them to say "thank you" when they receive something; it's about cultivating a heart of gratitude that sees God's hand in everything, even the small, everyday blessings.

Consider the common scenario of children constantly asking for the latest toys or technology, influenced by their peers or advertisements. It's easy for them to equate happiness with acquiring more things. However, as fathers, we can redirect their focus by modeling gratitude in our own lives. If we are thankful for what we have and express that gratitude regularly, our children will begin to understand that contentment doesn't come from having the latest gadget but from appreciating the blessings God has already provided.

Gratitude is more than an outward expression—it's a mindset. Teaching your children to be grateful begins with helping them recognize God's provision in their lives, both big and small. This can be as simple as giving thanks for a meal, acknowledging the beauty of creation during a family walk, or pointing out how God provides for your family's needs each day.

One way to instill gratitude is by emphasizing experiences over things. Children often remember moments spent together as a family far more than they remember the toys they've received. Taking the time to create meaningful family traditions—like family meals, weekend outings, or reading Scripture together—can foster a sense of appreciation for the things that matter most: relationships and faith. These moments help children see that God's blessings come in many forms, not just material possessions.

Gratitude can also be cultivated through serving others. When children learn to give, they begin to understand the value of what they have. Consider taking your children to volunteer at a local shelter, or participate in a church outreach project. These experiences open their eyes to the needs of others and can spark thankfulness for their own blessings. It also teaches them that they are blessed to be a blessing, reinforcing a sense of responsibility to share their gifts with others.

Another practical way to teach gratitude is through consistent acknowledgment of God's blessings. This can be done through daily prayers of thanks or starting a family gratitude journal where each member writes down things they are thankful for each day. This practice encourages your children to look for the good in their lives and reminds them that every good gift comes from God (James 1:17).

It's also essential to acknowledge that teaching gratitude takes time and patience. As fathers, we may feel frustrated when our children don't immediately grasp the importance of thankfulness, especially when surrounded by a world that often encourages the opposite. However, consistent modeling and intentional teaching will gradually help our children develop hearts that appreciate God's goodness in every aspect of life.

As you guide your children in this area, remember that gratitude isn't just about focusing on what we have; it's also about trusting God in what we don't have. When we model contentment, even in seasons of lack or difficulty, we show our children that our trust and joy are in God, not in our circumstances. This is the kind of gratitude that transforms hearts and families, fostering a lasting sense of peace and joy.

Action Step

Here are a few practical steps to help cultivate gratitude in your children this week:

1. **Start a Family Gratitude Journal**: Set aside time each day to have each family member write down one thing they are thankful for. This simple practice helps everyone focus on the blessings in their lives, whether big or small. At the end of the week, review the journal together and thank God for His provision.

2. **Model Gratitude in Everyday Conversations**: Make a point to express thankfulness regularly in front of your children. Whether you're thanking God for the meal on the table, appreciating the weather, or acknowledging a blessing at

work, let your children see you practicing gratitude in your daily life. This will teach them to do the same.

3. **Engage in a Family Service Project**: Find a way to serve others as a family. This could be donating food to a shelter, visiting a nursing home, or participating in a church outreach event. When children see the needs of others, it helps them appreciate the blessings they often take for granted. Serving together also creates meaningful family experiences that foster a spirit of gratitude.

By taking these steps, you can help your children develop a grateful heart and cultivate an attitude of thankfulness that lasts a lifetime.

Closing Prayer

Dear Heavenly Father, Thank You for the countless blessings You have given us. Help me as a father to model a heart of gratitude before my children. Teach me to see Your goodness in every situation and to express thankfulness in both the big and small moments of life. Lord, I pray that You would instill in my children a spirit of gratitude, that they may recognize Your provision and be content with what they have. Help us to be a family that gives thanks in all circumstances, trusting that You are always working for our good. Let our gratitude overflow into how we live and how we love others. In Jesus' name, we pray. Amen.

Week 25: Embracing Imperfections

"But he said to me, 'My grace is sufficient for you, for my power is made perfect in weakness.' Therefore I will boast all the more gladly about my weaknesses, so that Christ's power may rest on me." (2 Corinthians 12:9, NIV)

Reflection

As fathers, we often feel the pressure to be perfect in every aspect of life—providing for our families, raising our children with wisdom, and being spiritual leaders in the home. But despite our best efforts, we inevitably fall short. We make mistakes, say things we regret, and struggle to meet the expectations we place on ourselves. The challenge of embracing our imperfections is a tough one, especially in a world that expects perfection in every role we fill.

2 Corinthians 12:9 gives us a profound truth: God's power is made perfect in our weakness. When we feel inadequate as fathers, it's an opportunity to lean into God's grace rather than our strength. Being a father does not mean having all the answers or always getting it right. It means relying on God's strength and grace in the areas where we are weak.

Consider moments where you have felt frustrated or overwhelmed in your role as a father—whether it's losing your temper, feeling disconnected from your children, or not knowing how to guide them spiritually. These moments of imperfection can feel heavy, but they don't define your success as a father. Instead, they remind you of your need for God's guidance. When we try to carry the weight of fatherhood on our own, we are bound to stumble, but when we surrender our weaknesses to God, we give Him the space to work through us.

The pressure to be the "perfect dad" is a burden you don't have to bear. God doesn't expect perfection from you—He expects you to lean on Him. Through the humility of acknowledging where you fall short, you allow God's grace to fill the gaps. This not only gives you peace but also sets a powerful example for your children. They need to see that perfection is not required for love or approval, and they will learn this when they see you embracing your own imperfections.

When you recognize your weaknesses and surrender them to God, you invite His power into your fatherhood journey. It's in these moments of surrender that you grow, and your children witness the beauty of grace in action. They learn that they, too, can bring their imperfections before God, knowing that His love is not based on performance but on grace.

Action Step

Here are a few practical steps to help you embrace your imperfections and grow in grace this week:

1. **Acknowledge Your Weaknesses**: Take a moment to reflect on one area where you feel inadequate as a father. It could be managing your temper, feeling disconnected from your children, or struggling to provide spiritual leadership. Write down this weakness and commit it to God in prayer, asking for His grace to guide you in this area.
2. **Be Honest with Your Children**: One of the most powerful things you can do as a father is to be transparent with your

children about your own struggles. If you've made a mistake or reacted poorly, take the time to apologize and explain that you're also learning and growing. This teaches your children the importance of grace, humility, and forgiveness.

3. **Invite God's Strength**: Make it a habit to start each day by inviting God's strength into your role as a father. Pray for wisdom, patience, and grace as you lead your family, acknowledging that you can't do it all on your own. Lean into the promise of 2 Corinthians 12:9, trusting that God's power is perfect in your weakness.

By practicing these steps, you will not only find peace in your imperfections, but you will also create a home where grace abounds, and your children will learn to rely on God's strength rather than their own.

Closing Prayer

Dear Heavenly Father, Thank You for reminding me that I don't have to be a perfect father to lead my family. Your grace is sufficient for me, and Your power is made perfect in my weaknesses. Help me to embrace my imperfections, knowing that You are working through them. Teach me to lean on You in areas where I fall short and to model humility and grace for my children. Lord, I ask for Your strength to guide me as I grow in this journey of fatherhood. Let my children see Your grace at work in me, and help them understand that they, too, can come to You with their imperfections. Thank You for Your love, which covers all my failures. In Jesus' name, I pray. Amen.

Week 26: Prioritizing Your Marriage

"Husbands, love your wives, just as Christ loved the church and gave himself up for her." (Ephesians 5:25, NIV)

Reflection

Balancing marriage and fatherhood is no easy task. With the demands of parenting, work, and daily responsibilities, it can be challenging to prioritize your relationship with your spouse. As fathers, we often focus so much on our role as providers and protectors that we may unintentionally neglect the bond with our spouse. Yet, Ephesians 5:25 calls husbands to love their wives in the same sacrificial way that Christ loves the church.

The beauty of this scripture is that it reminds us of the selflessness required in marriage. Christ's love for the church was not conditional or based on convenience—it was a love that required sacrifice, patience, and deep commitment. As fathers, we are called to model this same love in our marriages. This means making time for your spouse, even when life feels overwhelming.

It's easy to push your relationship with your spouse to the back burner when the demands of fatherhood seem never-ending. Perhaps you've found yourself exhausted after a long day, struggling to find the energy to invest in your marriage. Maybe you've experienced moments of distance, where the connection you once had with your spouse feels diminished. These struggles are real, but they don't have to define your marriage.

Maintaining a strong marriage amidst the challenges of fatherhood is crucial, not just for your relationship but also for your children. When your kids see a healthy, loving relationship between their parents, they learn valuable lessons about love, respect, and partnership. Your marriage becomes a model for how they will approach relationships in their future.

While it may seem difficult to carve out time for your spouse, prioritizing your marriage is one of the most important investments you can make for your family. By leaning on God's grace and the wisdom found in scripture, you can strengthen the bond with your spouse and create a home where love, respect, and unity thrive.

Action Step

Here are a few actionable steps to help you prioritize your marriage this week:

1   **Plan a Special Time with Your Spouse**: This week, make an intentional effort to set aside time just for you and your spouse. It doesn't have to be elaborate—a simple date night at home or a walk together can make a big difference. The key is to focus on reconnecting and deepening your bond. Use this time to talk about your day, your dreams, or just enjoy each other's company without distractions.

2. **Pray Together**: Prayer is a powerful way to strengthen your marriage. If you haven't already, make it a habit to pray with your spouse daily. This can be as short as a few minutes before bed, asking God to guide your relationship, give you wisdom as parents, and help you show love and patience to one another.

3. **Show Acts of Kindness**: In the busyness of life, small acts of kindness often get overlooked. This week, intentionally show your spouse love through simple gestures—whether it's leaving a note of appreciation, helping with a task they usually do, or simply offering a listening ear. These small acts go a long way in nurturing a healthy and loving relationship.

By committing to these steps, you will not only strengthen your marriage but also create a stronger foundation for your family. Remember that marriage requires ongoing effort, but the rewards of a loving and supportive partnership will benefit both you and your children.

Closing Prayer

Dear Heavenly Father, Thank You for the gift of marriage and for the blessing of my spouse. Help me to prioritize my relationship with my spouse amidst the challenges of fatherhood. Give me the wisdom and strength to love selflessly, as Christ loves the church. Teach me to be patient, kind, and understanding, especially in moments of stress and fatigue. Lord, I pray for unity in my marriage, that my spouse and I may grow closer to each other and to You. Help us to model love and respect for our children, showing them what a healthy, God-centered marriage looks like. I ask for Your grace to strengthen our bond and for Your guidance in making time to nurture our relationship. In Jesus' name, I pray. Amen.

Week 27: Teaching Your Children to Trust in God

"Trust in the Lord with all your heart and lean not on your own understanding; in all your ways submit to Him, and He will make your paths straight." (Proverbs 3:5-6, NIV)

Daily Bible Reading

Sunday: Proverbs 3:5-6

Monday: Psalm 37:5

Tuesday: Jeremiah 17:7-8

Wednesday: Isaiah 26:3-4

Thursday: Matthew 6:25-34

Friday: Philippians 4:6-7

Saturday: Romans 15:13

Reflection

As fathers, one of our greatest desires is to see our children succeed, and it's tempting to teach them to rely on their talents, intellect, or strength. While self-confidence and responsibility are essential, teaching our children to trust in God's plan is even more important. Proverbs 3:5-6 reminds us that true wisdom comes from trusting in God's direction, not in our own understanding.

The world often encourages self-reliance, and it's easy for children to fall into this mindset, thinking they can solve every problem on their own. But as fathers, we must help them understand that faith in God is the foundation for a fulfilling life. It's not about abandoning their abilities, but about recognizing that their ultimate source of strength, wisdom, and guidance comes from God.

The struggle for many fathers is knowing how to instill this deep sense of trust in their children. We may worry that we are not spiritual enough ourselves or fear that our children may not understand the importance of relying on God. These concerns are real, but as Proverbs 3:5-6 teaches, we are to submit to God and trust His guidance, both for ourselves and for our children.

As you guide your children through life's challenges, model what it means to trust in God's plan. When they see you praying over decisions, seeking God's wisdom, and walking in faith, they learn to do the same. Trusting God doesn't mean avoiding hard work or responsibility, but rather acknowledging that God's plans are greater than our own.

Teach your children that trusting God involves surrendering control and embracing His promises, even when they don't immediately see the outcome. Whether they face academic challenges, peer pressure, or personal struggles, remind them that God's path for them is filled with hope and purpose.

Action Step

Here are a few practical steps you can take this week to help your children learn to trust in God:

1. **Share a Personal Story of Trust**: Take time this week to share with your children a story from your own life where you had to trust God, even when the outcome was uncertain. Be open about your fears or doubts, and explain how God's faithfulness helped you through the situation. This personal example can serve as a powerful lesson for them.
2. **Pray Together for Guidance**: As a family, come together in prayer and ask God for wisdom in a particular area of your lives. Whether it's a decision about school, friendships, or another challenge, show your children the importance of seeking God's guidance in every part of life.

3. **Encourage Trust Over Worry**: Help your children recognize when they are anxious or trying to control things on their own. Teach them to replace worry with trust by turning to God in prayer and remembering His promises. Make it a habit to remind them that God is in control, and they don't have to carry their burdens alone.

By taking these simple steps, you create an environment where your children learn that trusting God is not just a concept but a daily practice. Your example as a father plays a key role in shaping their faith journey.

Closing Prayer

Dear Heavenly Father, Thank You for the gift of fatherhood and the opportunity to guide my children in their faith journey. Help me to teach them the value of trusting You in all things, knowing that Your plans are greater than ours. Lord, I ask for wisdom as I guide them through the challenges they face. Help me to model what it means to lean on You and to submit to Your will, even when life feels uncertain. Please strengthen my children's faith, and may they grow to trust You with all their hearts. In moments of doubt or fear, remind them of Your promises and fill their hearts with peace. Thank You for Your constant guidance and love. In Jesus' name, I pray. Amen.

Week 28: Handling Disappointment in Fatherhood

"And we know that in all things God works for the good of those who love him, who have been called according to his purpose."

(Romans 8:28, NIV)

Daily Bible Reading

Sunday: Romans 8:28

Monday: Proverbs 19:21

Tuesday: Psalm 34:18

Wednesday: Isaiah 55:8-9

Thursday: Jeremiah 29:11

Friday: Psalm 37:23-24

Saturday: James 1:2-4

Reflection

As fathers, we often have expectations for ourselves, our children, and our families. We hope to lead them well, to see them thrive, and to manage all the demands of life smoothly. However, life frequently presents moments where these expectations go unmet, leading to feelings of disappointment. It could be a failed career decision, struggles in a child's behavior, or the simple reality that life isn't turning out the way we envisioned.

In those moments, the weight of disappointment can feel overwhelming. We may question our abilities, wonder if we've failed as fathers, or even begin to doubt our purpose in leading our families. Yet, Romans 8:28 offers profound reassurance: God is working for our good, even in the disappointments. His plan is greater than what we can see, and His purposes are always unfolding, even when we face setbacks.

Understanding that God uses all circumstances for His purposes can reshape how we view disappointment. It's not a sign of failure but an opportunity to trust in His greater plan. Disappointment in fatherhood, whether it's from unmet expectations in our parenting or from life's challenges, invites us to lean deeper into faith. It's a chance to let go of control and trust that God is guiding our families in ways we may not yet understand.

Fathers often feel the pressure to fix everything and make sure their families are always on track, but this isn't a burden we are meant to carry alone. When we submit our disappointments to God, we find that He not only brings peace but also works through these moments to strengthen us and refine our character. As fathers, we can model this trust in God for our children, teaching them that while life may not always go as planned, God's purpose is always good and His timing perfect.

Real-life examples show how fathers face disappointments both big and small—from a lost job to a strained relationship with a teenager—and yet, these moments can lead to growth when entrusted to God. Through these experiences, we can show our children how to navigate life's inevitable disappointments with faith, resilience, and hope.

Action Step

Here are a few practical steps you can take this week to handle disappointment in fatherhood:

1. **Reflect and Release**: Take a moment to reflect on a recent disappointment you've experienced as a father. Maybe it's related to your child's behavior, your own struggles, or a situation beyond your control. Write down how this disappointment has affected you and release it to God in prayer. Ask Him to help you see His purpose in it and give you peace.

2. **Discuss with Your Family**: Have an open conversation with your spouse or children about how they handle disappointment. Share your own experiences and model vulnerability by admitting that things don't always go the way you expect. This can be a teaching moment to show how trusting in God's plan can bring peace even in difficult circumstances.

3. **Focus on God's Promises**: Throughout the week, meditate on Romans 8:28 and other scriptures that remind you of God's faithfulness. When feelings of disappointment arise, pause and turn to these verses as reminders that God is always working for your good, even in the setbacks.

By taking these steps, you will not only handle your own disappointments with more grace, but you'll also demonstrate to your children how to navigate life's ups and downs with faith. Let them see that trusting God's bigger picture brings hope and resilience, even when things don't go as planned.

Closing Prayer

Heavenly Father, Thank You for Your promise in Romans 8:28, that You work all things for good for those who love You. I bring before You the disappointments I have faced as a father, and I release them into Your hands. Help me to trust in Your perfect plan, even when life doesn't go the way I expect. Grant me peace in the moments of unmet expectations and guide me to see Your purpose in every circumstance. Strengthen my faith as I lead my family, and help me model resilience and trust in You for my children. Thank You for always being with me, turning even the hardest moments into opportunities for growth and grace. In Jesus' name, I pray. Amen.

Week 29: Creating Family Traditions of Faith

"In the future, when your children ask you, 'What do these stones mean?' tell them that the flow of the Jordan was cut off before the ark of the covenant of the Lord. When it crossed the Jordan, the waters of the Jordan were cut off. These stones are to be a memorial to the people of Israel forever." (Joshua 4:6-7, NIV)

Daily Bible Reading

Sunday: Joshua 4:6-7

Monday: Deuteronomy 6:6-9

Tuesday: Psalm 78:4-7

Wednesday: Proverbs 22:6

Thursday: 2 Timothy 1:5

Friday: Matthew 7:24-27

Saturday: Exodus 12:24-27

Reflection

As fathers, one of our most important tasks is passing down our faith to our children. In a world full of distractions, creating strong family traditions rooted in faith helps solidify the foundation for future generations. Traditions give our families anchors, something tangible they can return to during times of doubt, joy, or hardship.

Joshua 4:6-7 shows us the power of memorials in remembering God's faithfulness. After the Israelites crossed the Jordan River, God instructed them to set up stones as a reminder of His mighty work. These stones served as physical markers, sparking questions from future generations and allowing fathers to share stories of God's intervention and provision. Similarly, the traditions we create in our homes today can serve as markers that point our children back to God's love and guidance.

Fathers often face the challenge of balancing busy schedules with spiritual leadership. It can feel overwhelming to establish faith-based traditions in the midst of work, school activities, and family life. However, it's crucial to remember that these traditions don't have to be elaborate. Whether it's praying together before meals, setting aside time for family devotions, or serving in a ministry together, what matters most is consistency and intentionality.

Take a moment to reflect on your own family's traditions. Are they grounded in faith, or do they focus more on entertainment and materialism? If you haven't yet established faith-based traditions, now is a great time to start. Perhaps begin by reading the Bible together as a family or praying before bedtime. In these moments, you are planting seeds that will grow into deep spiritual roots.

Real-life examples show how families that emphasize traditions of faith see long-lasting spiritual growth. Even something as simple as lighting candles on Sundays to represent Christ's light or creating a family gratitude journal can leave a profound impact on your children's faith journey. These small, intentional actions demonstrate the centrality of faith in your home and encourage your children to carry these practices into their future families.

Traditions not only teach our children about God but also create a bond within the family. In the busyness of life, setting aside specific moments to engage in spiritual activities as a family can strengthen your connection with one another and with God. It provides a space for fathers to model faith in action and show the importance of prioritizing God in everyday life.

Action Steps

Here are some practical steps to help you implement this week's lesson and create faith-based traditions in your family:

1. **Start a Weekly Family Devotion**: Set aside one night each week where the entire family gathers to read Scripture, discuss

a Bible story, or share how they've seen God at work in their lives. This regular gathering will help everyone grow in faith together and foster deeper spiritual conversations.

2. **Celebrate Faith Milestones**: Consider marking spiritual milestones like baptisms, confirmations, or answered prayers. This could be as simple as having a special dinner or writing in a family journal to reflect on how God has worked in your family's life. By celebrating these moments, you reinforce God's faithfulness and encourage your children to remember these milestones as part of their faith journey.

3. **Create a Family Prayer Tradition**: Develop a routine where the family prays together each day or week. This could be before bedtime, after dinner, or even on the way to school. Encourage each family member to share prayer requests and thank God for His blessings. This helps children learn the importance of relying on God in all aspects of life.

These steps are simple yet powerful ways to create lasting traditions that not only strengthen your family's bond but also deepen your children's relationship with God. Begin with one tradition and build on it as you feel led. Small, consistent practices are what will leave a lasting legacy of faith in your home.

Closing Prayer

Heavenly Father, thank You for the privilege of leading my family in faith. Help me to establish meaningful traditions that reflect Your love and truth. Teach me how to guide my children toward a deeper understanding of who You are and what You've done in our lives. I ask for Your wisdom in building a home centered on Your Word, where faith is practiced, remembered, and passed down through generations. Strengthen our family bonds as we draw closer to You, and may our traditions be a testimony of Your faithfulness. In Jesus' name, Amen.

Week 30: Handling Criticism as a Father

"Whoever heeds life-giving correction will be at home among the wise. Those who disregard discipline despise themselves, but the one who heeds correction gains understanding."

(Proverbs 15:31-32, NIV)

Daily Bible Reading

Sunday: Proverbs 15:31-32
Monday: James 1:19
Tuesday: Proverbs 12:1
Wednesday: Matthew 7:3-5
Thursday: Ephesians 4:29
Friday: Proverbs 19:20
Saturday: Romans 14:10

Reflection

As a father, it's inevitable that you will face criticism regarding your parenting decisions. Whether it comes from family members, friends, or even strangers, hearing others weigh in on how you raise your children can stir up feelings of doubt, frustration, or even anger. It can be especially tough when criticism comes from those closest to you, as their opinions often carry more weight.

Proverbs 15:31-32 offers us wisdom on how to handle criticism. It reminds us that life-giving correction leads to wisdom and growth, but rejecting it only hinders our ability to improve. As fathers, there are times when criticism, especially the constructive kind, can be an opportunity to reflect and grow in our parenting. However, we must also learn to distinguish between helpful advice and unnecessary negativity.

Fathers can often feel pressure to "get it right" in every situation, making them sensitive to critiques of their parenting. It's important to remember that no one is a perfect parent. Mistakes happen, and learning from those mistakes is part of the journey. At the same time, it's crucial to recognize when criticism is more harmful than helpful. Some people may offer opinions that are based on personal biases or misunderstandings of your family's unique dynamics. In such cases, it's vital to let go of those unhelpful opinions and focus on what truly matters: raising your children in a way that aligns with God's guidance.

Real-life examples show how fathers experience both constructive criticism and unfair judgments. A father may be told he's too strict or not strict enough. He may hear comments about his choices regarding his children's education, discipline, or even spiritual upbringing. It's easy to get caught up in these critiques, but it's essential to take a step back, seek God's wisdom, and ask yourself, "Is there something here I can learn from?" If the answer is yes, take the feedback to heart and apply it. If the answer is no, release it to God and move forward with confidence in your role as a father.

Ultimately, we are called to parent with humility, being open to learning and growth, while also trusting that God will guide us in our decisions. Don't let fear of criticism paralyze your actions. Instead, pray for discernment and the strength to remain steadfast in the face of negative feedback.

Action Steps

Here are some practical steps to help you handle criticism as a father and grow from the experience:

1. **Pray for Discernment**: Before reacting to any criticism, take a moment to pray for discernment. Ask God to reveal whether the critique is something you can learn from or if it's an opinion you need to let go of. Trust in His guidance to help you see the situation clearly.

2. **Evaluate the Criticism**: Take an honest look at the feedback you receive. Is there truth in what's being said? If so, reflect on how you can improve in that area. If the criticism is unfair or based on misunderstandings, remind yourself that not all opinions are worth dwelling on. Ask yourself: Does this align with God's will for how I parent?

3. **Respond with Grace**: Whether the feedback is constructive or not, strive to respond with grace. If the person offering criticism is well-meaning, thank them for their input and consider how you can apply it. If the feedback is hurtful or unnecessary, choose not to engage in defensiveness or anger. Instead, silently release it to God, and let His peace fill your heart.

By practicing these steps, you can approach criticism with humility and wisdom, using it as an opportunity to grow while also protecting your heart from unhelpful opinions. These actions not only strengthen your ability to handle criticism but also set a powerful example for your children on how to deal with feedback gracefully.

Closing Prayer

Heavenly Father, I come before You with a humble heart, asking for wisdom and strength in facing criticism as a father. Help me to discern the feedback that will help me grow and let go of the opinions that weigh me down unnecessarily. Teach me to respond with grace, even when I feel misunderstood, and to trust in Your guidance over my parenting decisions.

Lord, I ask for patience and humility as I seek to be the best father I can be. Remind me that I do not need to be perfect but to rely on You for wisdom and strength. In Jesus' name, I pray, Amen.

Week 31: Dealing with Comparison

"Each one should test their own actions. Then they can take pride in themselves alone, without comparing themselves to someone else, for each one should carry their own load."

(Galatians 6:4-5, NIV)

<table>
<tr><td colspan="2" align="center">Daily Bible Reading</td></tr>
<tr><td>Sunday: Galatians 6:4-5</td><td>Thursday: 2 Corinthians 10:12</td></tr>
<tr><td>Monday: Psalm 139:13-14</td><td>Friday: Philippians 2:3</td></tr>
<tr><td>Tuesday: 1 Corinthians 12:4-6</td><td>Saturday: Matthew 25:14-30</td></tr>
<tr><td>Wednesday: Romans 12:6</td><td></td></tr>
</table>

Reflection

As fathers, we often find ourselves silently comparing our parenting skills, successes, and even failures to other dads. Whether it's the dad who always seems to have it all together or the one whose kids are excelling in school, it's easy to feel inadequate. Social media, family gatherings, or even casual conversations with other fathers can stir up thoughts like, "Am I doing enough for my kids?" or "Why does that dad seem more successful than me?"

Galatians 6:4-5 offers an important reminder to focus on our own unique calling and responsibilities. The verse emphasizes testing our own actions rather than constantly measuring ourselves against others. Every father's journey is different. God has given each of us our own set of strengths and challenges, and our success is not defined by how we compare to someone else but by how we fulfill the role God has assigned us.

The temptation to compare often comes from a place of insecurity, where we question our abilities and feel as though we are falling short. But God sees the unique gifts and talents He has placed in each of us. The father who excels in one area may struggle in another, just as we do. Realizing that we are not meant to be identical to other dads helps relieve the pressure of comparison.

For instance, you may excel at teaching your children patience, while another dad is great at encouraging physical fitness. Instead of dwelling on where you think you're lacking, focus on the strengths you already bring to your family. Maybe it's the way you provide emotional support or how you demonstrate love and compassion. Trust that God has equipped you with what you need to lead your family.

Comparison can rob us of the joy of fatherhood. When we focus too much on how we measure up to others, we miss the blessings that come from simply being present and engaged in our own unique journey as a father. Instead of looking at others, fix your eyes on the calling God has placed on your life and take pride in fulfilling it to the best of your ability.

Action Steps

Here are some practical steps to help you overcome the temptation to compare yourself to other fathers:

1. **Focus on Your Strengths**: Each father has a unique set of skills and qualities. Take some time to reflect on what you do well as a dad. It could be your ability to listen, your patience, or your sense of humor. Write down one strength that you bring to your family and thank God for it. Remember, God has equipped you to fulfill your specific role.
2. **Limit Comparison Triggers**: Social media and casual conversations can sometimes trigger feelings of inadequacy. If scrolling through your feed or hearing about other dads'

successes makes you feel less than, it might be time to take a break. Instead, spend that time focusing on strengthening your relationship with your kids and building your own family culture.

3. **Pray for Contentment**: Comparison often stems from discontentment. Spend time in prayer asking God to help you be content with who you are as a father and to trust that He has a unique plan for you and your family. Thank Him for the specific ways He has equipped you to lead your children.

These steps can help you redirect your energy away from comparison and toward gratitude and growth. The more you focus on the unique gifts God has given you, the more you'll appreciate the father you are becoming.

Closing Prayer

Heavenly Father, I come to You today, asking for Your help in overcoming the temptation to compare myself to other fathers. I know that You have created me with a unique purpose and that You have given me everything I need to fulfill my role as a dad. Help me to focus on the strengths You have placed within me and to trust in Your guidance as I lead my family.

Lord, when I feel inadequate or fall into the trap of comparison, remind me that my worth comes from You, not from how I measure up to others. Teach me to find contentment in the father You've called me to be, and to take pride in the work You are doing in me. Thank You for the gifts You have entrusted to me and for the opportunity to lead my children. Help me to lead with confidence, grace, and wisdom. In Jesus' name, I pray, Amen.

Week 32: Encouraging Spiritual Growth in Your Children

"Start children off on the way they should go, and even when they are old they will not turn from it." (Proverbs 22:6, NIV)

Daily Bible Reading

Sunday: Proverbs 22:6

Monday: Deuteronomy 6:6-7

Tuesday: Psalm 78:4-7

Wednesday: Ephesians 6:4

Thursday: 2 Timothy 1:5

Friday: Colossians 3:16

Saturday: Matthew 19:14

Reflection

As a father, one of the greatest challenges can be feeling inadequate when it comes to your children's spiritual growth. We often wonder, "Am I doing enough to teach them about God?" or "What if I don't know the answers to their questions about faith?" These uncertainties can burden our hearts, particularly in a world full of distractions and conflicting influences.

Proverbs 22:6 reminds us that our role as fathers is to "start children off on the way they should go," trusting that as they grow, God will continue the work we've begun. This verse encourages us to take the first steps, knowing that God will guide our children long after our daily influence. While it can feel overwhelming to carry the responsibility of shaping their faith, we must remember that we are not alone in this journey.

Fostering spiritual growth in children is not about being perfect or having all the answers; it's about consistently modeling faith and trust in God. Whether it's praying with your children, reading Scripture together, or talking about how God is at work in your own life, these small daily moments of faithfulness plant seeds that God will nurture in their hearts.

For instance, you might feel like you're not a Bible scholar or you're unsure how to explain complex theological concepts, but the truth is, your children will learn more from your everyday example of faith than from any textbook answer. If they see you turning to God in prayer, trusting Him during challenges, and prioritizing time with Him, they will understand that faith is an active and integral part of life.

Ultimately, trust that God is at work in your children's hearts. Your role is to provide guidance and encouragement, while God does the transformative work. When you feel inadequate, lean on Him, knowing that He is the one who brings growth.

Action Steps

Here are a few practical ways to foster spiritual growth in your children this week:

1. **Set a Regular Prayer or Devotion Time**: Establish a consistent time each day or week for spiritual discussion, prayer, or Bible reading as a family. This doesn't have to be long or complicated—just a few minutes of talking about a Bible verse or praying together can have a lasting impact.
2. **Incorporate Faith into Daily Life**: Use everyday moments to point out God's work in the world. For example, when your children face challenges at school or home, remind them of God's presence and encourage them to pray. Show them that faith is relevant in every aspect of life.
3. **Model Transparency in Your Own Walk with God**: Don't be afraid to let your children see your own spiritual journey—both the highs and the struggles. If they see that you don't have all the answers but are seeking God, they will learn that faith is a lifelong process of growth and trust.

By incorporating these simple practices, you create an environment where spiritual conversations are natural and consistent. Trust that God will honor your efforts as you guide your children toward Him.

Closing Prayer

Dear Heavenly Father, I come to You today asking for wisdom and guidance as I lead my children in their spiritual growth. I often feel inadequate or unsure, but I trust in Your promise that as I lead them in Your ways, You will continue the work in their hearts. Help me to be faithful in teaching them about You and to model a life of trust and faith in You.

Lord, give me the courage to share my own walk with You, the wisdom to answer their questions, and the patience to guide them as they grow. Help me to remember that it is You who brings true growth and transformation in their hearts.

Thank You for entrusting me with the responsibility of guiding my children toward You. I commit their spiritual journey to Your care and ask that You would lead them every step of the way. In Jesus' name, Amen.

Week 33: Managing Work Stress

"Come to me, all you who are weary and burdened, and I will give you rest." (Matthew 11:28, NIV)

Reflection

As a father, the responsibilities of providing for your family can often create stress, especially when work pressures build up. Many fathers find it difficult to leave the burdens of their job at the door when they come home. Whether it's a project deadline, an issue with a colleague, or financial concerns, work stress can spill into family life, affecting your mood and interactions with your spouse and children.

Matthew 11:28 offers a simple yet profound solution: "Come to me, all you who are weary and burdened, and I will give you rest." Jesus invites us to bring our burdens to Him, including the stress that comes from work. It's a reminder that we don't have to carry everything on our own.

As fathers, it's easy to feel like we need to be strong and hold everything together, but trying to manage stress without turning to God can lead to emotional burnout, irritability, and strained relationships at home. The pressure to be everything for everyone at work and at home can overwhelm even the strongest men. But Jesus promises rest for our souls when we lay our burdens at His feet.

Imagine coming home after a stressful day, your mind still racing with thoughts of unfinished work. Instead of walking into your house carrying that weight, take five minutes in your car to pray and ask God to take your worries. When you step through the door, you're entering a sanctuary, a place where you can focus on being present for your family. The peace that comes from handing over your stress to God allows you to be the husband and father your family needs.

It's important to remember that while work is necessary, your family is your primary ministry. By learning to manage stress and trust God with your burdens, you can create a more peaceful home environment where you're fully present for your loved ones.

Action Step

Here are a few practical ways to manage work-related stress and ensure it doesn't affect your time with your family:

1. **Take Five Minutes for Prayer After Work**: Before walking through the door, spend five minutes in your car or a quiet place praying and handing over your stress to God. Ask Him to take away the burdens of the day and fill you with peace as you step into your home. This small habit can make a huge difference in your mindset and attitude when you engage with your family.

2. **Set Boundaries for Work and Family Time**: Make a commitment to set clear boundaries between work and home life. Once you're home, avoid checking emails or answering work-related calls unless absolutely necessary. Use this time to focus solely on your family, creating a healthy balance between work responsibilities and family connections.

3. **Create a Stress-Relief Routine**: Find a simple activity that helps you unwind from work stress. It could be a short walk after work, deep breathing exercises, or listening to worship music. By developing a routine to release tension, you'll be better equipped to leave your work stress behind and enjoy time with your family.

By incorporating these practical steps, you can honor both your work responsibilities and your role as a father without allowing stress to dominate your time with your family.

Closing Prayer

Heavenly Father, I come to You today, asking for Your help as I navigate the stress and burdens of work. I know that You invite me to bring all my worries to You, and so I ask for Your peace to fill my heart. Help me to release the burdens of my job and trust You to handle what I cannot.

Lord, I ask for Your strength to set aside the pressures of work when I'm with my family. Teach me to be fully present with my spouse and children, showing them love and attention. Remind me that my home is a place of rest and connection, and that You will provide for every need.

Thank You for the gift of my family and for the peace that comes from trusting in You. Guide me as I lead them and help me to model Your love and patience, even during stressful times. In Jesus' name, Amen.

Week 34: Fostering a Spirit of Service in Your Family

"For even the Son of Man did not come to be served, but to serve, and to give his life as a ransom for many." (Mark 10:45, NIV)

Daily Bible Reading

Sunday: Mark 10:45

Monday: Philippians 2:3-4

Tuesday: Galatians 5:13

Wednesday: Matthew 25:35-40

Thursday: John 13:14-15

Friday: Romans 12:10

Saturday: Colossians 3:23-24

Reflection

As fathers, one of the greatest lessons we can teach our children is the value of serving others. In a world that often promotes self-centeredness, we have a higher calling to follow the example of Christ, who "did not come to be served, but to serve." (Mark 10:45, NIV) Jesus modeled what true servanthood looks like, demonstrating humility, love, and selflessness in every aspect of His life. As fathers, we have the opportunity to reflect that same spirit of service in our homes and encourage our children to do the same.

It's not always easy. We often face the challenge of balancing our own responsibilities—work, family, finances—and may feel overwhelmed by the thought of taking on more. Teaching our children to serve can seem like one more task in an already packed schedule. But fostering a heart of service isn't about adding something extra; it's about infusing a mindset of generosity and kindness into the everyday moments of life.

Children naturally learn by watching their parents. When they see their father offer help to a neighbor, give time to those in need, or simply serve in the household without grumbling, they begin to understand what it means to live out Christ's example. But modeling service isn't just about actions; it's also about cultivating the right attitude. Service rooted in love, as Philippians 2:3-4 reminds us, comes from a place of humility and a desire to lift others up rather than seeking personal gain.

A father's role in fostering this heart of service involves encouraging small, consistent acts of kindness that gradually build into a lifestyle of servanthood. It may be as simple as asking your children to help an elderly neighbor or contributing to a family service project. Over time, these small acts will leave a lasting imprint on their hearts, teaching them to value others above themselves, just as Jesus did.

Action Step

Here are a few practical steps you can take to instill a spirit of service in your family:

1. **Plan a Family Service Project**: This week, sit down with your family and plan a service project you can all participate in together. It could be as simple as visiting a nursing home, volunteering at a local food bank, or helping a neighbor with yard work. Involve your children in choosing the project so they feel ownership in the act of service.
2. **Incorporate Service into Daily Life**: Service doesn't have to be a big event. Find small ways to serve each other within the home. Assign tasks where your children help each other out, like a sibling helping to clean up after a meal or taking on a chore to lighten someone else's load. These small acts of kindness can build a culture of service in the home.

3. **Lead by Example**: Let your children see you serving others, both in and outside the home. Whether it's offering help to someone at church, taking on a volunteer role, or simply being attentive to the needs of family members, your actions will speak louder than words. Children often mirror the behaviors they see, so showing them what a servant's heart looks like is key to teaching this value.

By focusing on these simple but meaningful steps, you can foster a spirit of service in your children that will impact their lives and the lives of those around them for years to come.

Closing Prayer

Heavenly Father, thank You for the perfect example of service that Your Son, Jesus, set for us. Help me as a father to model that same spirit of service in my home and in my daily life. Teach me to serve with humility and love, not seeking recognition but desiring to honor You in all that I do.

Lord, I pray for my children, that they may grow to understand the joy that comes from serving others. Instill in their hearts a desire to help those around them, and guide me as I teach them the value of putting others before themselves.

As we strive to serve one another, let our actions reflect Your love and grace. Give us the strength and wisdom to create a family that is rooted in kindness and generosity. In Jesus' name, I pray. Amen.

Week 35: Teaching Your Children to Forgive

"For if you forgive other people when they sin against you, your heavenly Father will also forgive you. But if you do not forgive others their sins, your Father will not forgive your sins."

(Matthew 6:14-15, NIV)

Daily Bible Reading

Sunday: Matthew 6:14-15

Monday: Colossians 3:13

Tuesday: Ephesians 4:32

Wednesday: Luke 6:37

Thursday: 1 Peter 4:8

Friday: Mark 11:25

Saturday: Matthew 18:21-22

Reflection

One of the hardest lessons to teach our children is forgiveness, especially in a world that often emphasizes revenge and holding grudges. Yet, forgiveness is at the core of the Christian faith. As fathers, our role in guiding our children to understand the importance of forgiving others is crucial for their emotional and spiritual health. Forgiveness isn't about excusing bad behavior, but about freeing ourselves from the burden of resentment and bitterness.

In Matthew 6:14-15, Jesus teaches that our willingness to forgive others mirrors God's forgiveness toward us. It's a powerful reminder that if we expect God's grace, we must extend grace to others. This principle can be challenging for children to grasp, especially when they feel wronged by a sibling, friend, or even a parent. But the ability to forgive is essential in nurturing healthy relationships, both within the family and beyond.

Real-life scenarios often involve moments when our children feel hurt—perhaps a sibling took their toy or a friend said something unkind. These instances, though small, are opportunities to teach a greater truth: that holding onto anger only hurts us in the end. We, as fathers, need to lead by example, showing them how to let go of offenses and seek peace. When children witness their father apologizing or forgiving someone, they begin to internalize the value of forgiveness as a way of living.

Forgiveness does not come naturally; it must be practiced, especially in families. We are bound to hurt each other, sometimes unintentionally, but teaching our children to forgive quickly and fully allows them to experience the healing power that forgiveness brings. When forgiveness is present in the home, it paves the way for emotional healing and growth, reducing the sting of offenses and creating an atmosphere of love, understanding, and grace.

Action Step

Here are three actionable steps you can take this week to teach your children the importance of forgiveness:

1. **Start a Forgiveness Conversation**: Take time to talk with your children about forgiveness. Ask them about moments when they've been hurt or upset by others, and discuss how they felt. Then, share with them why God calls us to forgive and how forgiving others can bring peace to our hearts. Encourage them to think of someone they can forgive this week, whether it's a sibling, a friend, or even themselves.
2. **Lead by Example**: Show your children what forgiveness looks like by modeling it in your own life. If you've had an argument with your spouse or another family member, make it a point to reconcile and ask for forgiveness in front of your children. Let them see that even adults need to forgive and seek

forgiveness. This powerful example will leave a lasting impression.

3. **Practice Apologizing and Forgiving**: Create a practice within your family where, if someone is hurt or offended, they make a sincere effort to apologize and ask for forgiveness. Encourage the other party to respond with a forgiving heart. Reinforce that this doesn't mean the wrong action was okay, but that forgiveness allows healing to begin. This practice, over time, will help your children develop a habit of forgiveness.

By intentionally focusing on these steps, you will help instill a culture of forgiveness in your home, fostering stronger and healthier relationships.

Closing Prayer

Heavenly Father, thank You for the gift of forgiveness. Help me as a father to model Your grace and mercy in my own life so that I can teach my children the importance of forgiving others. Lord, I know that holding onto anger only harms us, but forgiving opens the door to healing and peace.

I pray for my children, that they may learn to forgive quickly and with a full heart. Guide me as I help them navigate the hurts they experience, and show them how to let go of bitterness and embrace the freedom that comes with forgiveness. Lord, may our home be filled with love, grace, and compassion, reflecting Your heart in all we do. In Jesus' name, I pray. Amen.

Week 36: Managing Expectations as a Father

"Be completely humble and gentle; be patient, bearing with one another in love." (Ephesians 4:2, NIV)

Reflection

As fathers, we want the best for our children. We see their potential and often hold high expectations for their behavior, accomplishments, and growth. But sometimes, these expectations can lead to frustration, both for us and for them. When our goals for them are too lofty or rigid, we risk placing undue pressure on their young hearts, hindering their unique journey.

Ephesians 4:2 reminds us to practice patience and gentleness in all our relationships, including with our children. As they grow and learn, they will make mistakes and face challenges. Our role as fathers is not to demand perfection but to guide them with love and understanding. It's easy to get caught up in wanting them to excel academically, athletically, or socially, but we must remember that God has a unique plan for each of our children. Our job is to nurture them, allowing space for them to grow at their own pace while encouraging them in their strengths.

Take, for instance, a father who has high academic expectations for his child. The child may struggle in a particular subject, leading to frustration on both sides. While the father's desire for the child to succeed is well-intentioned, the pressure can cause the child to feel inadequate. A better approach would be to support the child's learning process, offering encouragement and patience rather than focusing solely on the final result.

Balancing expectations with realistic goals is challenging. We want our children to strive for greatness, but we also need to be mindful of their individual growth, capabilities, and limitations. By practicing patience and humility, we can help them navigate their own journey without feeling overwhelmed by our desires for them.

Action Steps

Here are some practical steps you can take this week to better balance your expectations and support your child's unique path:

1. **Evaluate Your Expectations**: Take a moment to reflect on your current expectations for your child. Are they reasonable? Are they based on your desires or on what your child truly needs? Adjust your goals to better align with your child's strengths, weaknesses, and current stage of development. Remember, growth is a process, and every child's journey is different.
2. **Communicate with Your Child**: Have an open and honest conversation with your child about their goals and challenges. Listen to their thoughts and feelings about the expectations you've set for them. This dialogue will help you better understand where they need encouragement and where you might need to offer more patience.
3. **Celebrate Progress, Not Perfection**: Focus on celebrating small victories rather than waiting for your child to meet the final goal. Whether it's improving a skill or showing effort in a new area, acknowledge their hard work and determination.

This will build their confidence and motivate them to keep growing, knowing they have your full support.

By taking these steps, you can create a nurturing environment where your child feels supported in their unique journey, free from unrealistic pressures.

Closing Prayer

Heavenly Father, I come before You today, asking for Your guidance and wisdom as I navigate the responsibilities of fatherhood. Help me to balance my expectations for my children with patience and love. Remind me, Lord, that You have created each of them uniquely, with their own strengths, gifts, and timing.

Give me the humility to adjust my goals and the grace to walk alongside them as they grow. Help me to celebrate their progress and offer encouragement rather than frustration. Teach me to lead with gentleness, just as You lead me.

Lord, I hand over my desires for my children's future to You, trusting in Your plan for their lives. Help me to guide them in a way that honors You and strengthens our bond. In Jesus' name, I pray. Amen.

Week 37: Coping with Rejection

"As you come to him, the living Stone—rejected by humans but chosen by God and precious to him." (1 Peter 2:4, NIV)

Reflection

As fathers, one of the hardest feelings to bear is rejection, especially when it comes from those closest to us—our children or family members. Whether it's a rebellious teenager who pushes you away, or feeling undervalued in your own home, the pain of rejection can cut deep. It's in these moments we may question our worth as fathers and wonder if we're doing something wrong.

The scripture in 1 Peter 2:4 reminds us that even Jesus was rejected by the world, but He was precious and chosen by God. Despite the world's dismissal, Jesus found His identity and value in the Father's love. In the same way, we can rest in the assurance that our worth comes from God, not from the acceptance or approval of others. Just as Jesus was rejected yet remained beloved by His Father, we too are precious in God's eyes, even when we face rejection.

For fathers, rejection might look like a child who pulls away emotionally or defies your authority. It could be a spouse or extended family member who doesn't appreciate the efforts you make. These feelings can leave you feeling isolated, frustrated, and sometimes defeated. However, rejection is not a measure of your worth or abilities as a father.

In these tough moments, it's crucial to remember that rejection does not define you. God has chosen you to be a father, and He equips you for that role, even when it feels difficult. When we feel rejected, it's an opportunity to turn to God and seek comfort and affirmation in His love. His approval never wavers, and His love is constant.

Take, for example, a father whose teenage child seems distant and unresponsive. Despite his efforts to connect, the child continues to withdraw. While this situation may make the father feel like he's failing, he can take comfort in knowing that God sees his heart and his dedication. The rejection, painful as it is, does not mean he is not a good father—it's a part of the child's growth process, and God can use it for good.

Rejection, though painful, offers us a chance to deepen our trust in God. When we experience these moments, we can find refuge in God's unchanging love and remember that our identity is in Him, not in the opinions or responses of others.

Action Steps

Here are some practical steps you can take this week to handle feelings of rejection as a father:

1. **Reflect on Past Rejection**: Take some time to think about a specific moment where you felt rejected by your child or family member. Write it down and bring it to God in prayer, asking Him to help you find peace and comfort in His love rather than seeking validation from others.
2. **Affirm Your Identity in Christ**: Rejection often causes us to doubt ourselves. Spend time each day reminding yourself that

your worth comes from God. Use affirming scriptures, such as Romans 8:38-39, to reinforce your identity in Christ. Repeat these truths to yourself whenever you feel rejected or undervalued.

3. **Pray for Reconciliation**: While rejection is painful, it doesn't have to be permanent. Pray specifically for the relationship where you feel rejection, asking God to soften hearts and bring healing and reconciliation. Also, pray for the strength to continue loving unconditionally, just as God loves us.

By focusing on God's approval and trusting Him to work in your relationships, you can handle feelings of rejection with grace and find strength in His unwavering love.

Closing Prayer

Dear Heavenly Father, I come before You with a heavy heart, feeling the weight of rejection in my role as a father. I ask for Your comfort and peace in these moments. Help me to remember that my worth and value are found in You, not in the approval of others. Just as Your Son, Jesus, was rejected yet beloved, remind me that I am chosen and loved by You, even when I feel unappreciated or pushed aside.

Lord, give me the strength to continue loving my children and family unconditionally, even when they distance themselves from me. Soften their hearts, and bring reconciliation where it is needed. Help me to lead with grace and patience, trusting that You are working in their hearts and in mine.

Thank You, Father, for Your steadfast love that never fails. Help me to lean on You in times of rejection, knowing that I am always accepted and cherished by You. In Jesus' name, I pray. Amen.

Week 38: Honoring and Loving Your Wife

"Husbands, love your wives, just as Christ loved the church and gave himself up for her." (Ephesians 5:25, NIV)

Daily Bible Reading

Sunday: Ephesians 5:25

Monday: 1 Peter 3:7

Tuesday: Proverbs 31:10-12

Wednesday: Colossians 3:19

Thursday: Song of Solomon 2:10-11

Friday: Genesis 2:24

Saturday: Ecclesiastes 4:9-10

Reflection

Fatherhood is an incredible calling, but alongside this, there's another sacred role—being a loving and present husband. At times, it can be challenging to balance the responsibilities of both fatherhood and marriage. Between the duties of providing, parenting, and everyday life, it's easy for the marriage relationship to take a back seat.

Ephesians 5:25 reminds husbands of their divine calling to love their wives sacrificially, just as Christ loved the church. This is a high standard of love—one that requires patience, humility, and intentional care. Loving your wife is not just about fulfilling duties but about nurturing her emotionally, spiritually, and relationally.

As fathers, we often focus so much on our role as protectors and providers for our children that we can forget how vital our role is in our marriage. Our children watch us closely and learn about love, partnership, and respect through how we treat their mother. Honoring your wife, showing her love, and intentionally making time for her strengthens the entire family dynamic. It creates a home filled with love and sets a powerful example of what a healthy marriage looks like.

Every marriage faces challenges, whether it's the stress of balancing work, parenting, or dealing with life's uncertainties. However, it's crucial to remember that your wife is your partner in this journey. She is not just another responsibility on the list; she is your helper, your confidante, and the one you are called to love deeply.

Take some time this week to reflect on how you can better honor your wife. Whether it's through kind words, small acts of service, or simply being present, showing her love and respect is a way of fulfilling God's call to love her as Christ loves the church.

Action Steps

This week, focus on strengthening your relationship with your wife by taking these simple steps:

1. **Plan a Date Night**: Set aside time specifically for your wife this week, whether it's an evening out or a quiet night at home. The goal is to reconnect with her and focus solely on your relationship without distractions. Use this time to express your love, gratitude, and appreciation for her.
2. **Speak Words of Affirmation**: Throughout the week, make an intentional effort to speak life-giving words to your wife. Compliment her, thank her for what she does for your family, and remind her how much she means to you. These small gestures can have a big impact on her heart.
3. **Pray Together**: One of the most powerful ways to honor your wife is by covering her in prayer. Take time to pray with her and for her. Ask God to strengthen your bond, provide wisdom in your relationship, and help you both grow in love.

These actions will not only deepen your connection with your wife but also reflect the love and care that God desires for your marriage. Remember, your relationship with your wife is a foundation for the whole family, and nurturing it is part of being the husband and father God calls you to be.

Closing Prayer

Dear Lord, Thank You for the gift of my wife and for the love You have shown us through our marriage. I ask for Your guidance in helping me to love her as Christ loves the church. Teach me to honor her, to speak kindly, and to serve her with humility and grace.

Help me to prioritize our relationship amidst the many responsibilities of fatherhood. Strengthen our bond and show us how to support one another in this journey. Where there are struggles, grant us patience and understanding. Where there is joy, may we celebrate it together.

Lord, I pray that our marriage would reflect Your love and serve as a strong example to our children. Help me to lead my family with love, compassion, and a heart that seeks to glorify You in all things.   In Jesus' name, I pray. Amen.Week

Week 39: Supporting Your Wife Spiritually

"Therefore encourage one another and build each other up, just as in fact you are doing." (1 Thessalonians 5:11, NIV)

Reflection

As a father, you're called not only to guide your children but also to be a spiritual leader for your wife. This can sometimes be a challenge as you juggle the responsibilities of work, fatherhood, and your personal faith. However, providing spiritual support to your wife is a crucial part of your role as a husband.

1 Thessalonians 5:11 encourages us to build one another up and offer support and encouragement, especially in the context of faith. In marriage, your spiritual journey should be shared, helping one another grow closer to God. Supporting your wife's spiritual well-being requires being intentional about encouraging her in prayer, scripture reading, and seeking God's will in your lives together.

There may be times when your wife is facing spiritual struggles—perhaps dealing with doubt, fatigue, or simply feeling disconnected from God. During these moments, you have a unique opportunity to come alongside her, offer encouragement, and strengthen her faith.

Leading spiritually does not mean having all the answers, but it does mean being a source of support and prayer for your wife. It's about listening to her spiritual needs and walking alongside her in both the highs and lows. It's about helping her seek God in her life, fostering a home where spiritual growth is encouraged, and reminding her of God's faithfulness.

Make it a point to invest in her spiritual journey, just as you do in your children's. It may be something as simple as praying together, reading the Bible together, or asking about her relationship with God. The small efforts can have a profound impact on your marriage, strengthening not only your faith but also your bond as husband and wife.

Action Steps

1. **Pray Together Daily**: Set aside time to pray together as a couple each day. Whether it's in the morning, before meals, or at the end of the day, inviting God into your relationship through prayer strengthens the spiritual connection between you and your wife.
2. **Encourage Her Faith**: Find ways to encourage your wife in her faith journey. This could mean sending her a Bible verse that inspires you, listening to her spiritual concerns, or simply asking how you can pray for her. Show her that you value her spiritual growth and are there to support her.
3. **Attend Worship Together**: If possible, make attending worship together a priority. Whether it's church service, a Bible study, or a faith-based event, sharing moments of worship strengthens your relationship and keeps your focus on God as the center of your marriage.

These steps will help create an environment where both of you can grow spiritually, encouraging each other to seek God and lean on Him in every aspect of your lives. Leading by example in faith can inspire your wife and create a deeper sense of unity and purpose in your marriage.

Closing Prayer

Heavenly Father, Thank You for the blessing of my wife and the gift of our marriage. I ask for Your guidance as I seek to be a spiritual leader in our relationship. Help me to support her in her faith journey and to encourage her with love, patience, and understanding.

Lord, I pray that You would strengthen our bond through prayer, worship, and a shared desire to grow closer to You. Teach me to be attentive to her spiritual needs and to walk alongside her as we both seek to honor You in our lives together.

Please guide our marriage, protect it from distractions, and keep our hearts focused on You. May our home be filled with Your presence and peace, and may we always seek to glorify You in everything we do.

In Jesus' name, I pray. Amen.

Week 40: Avoiding and Resolving Conflict with Your Wife

"Do not let the sun go down while you are still angry."

(Ephesians 4:26, NIV)

<table>
<tr><td colspan="2" align="center">Daily Bible Reading</td></tr>
<tr><td>Sunday: Ephesians 4:26</td><td>Thursday: Matthew 5:23-24</td></tr>
<tr><td>Monday: Proverbs 15:1</td><td>Friday: Romans 12:18</td></tr>
<tr><td>Tuesday: Colossians 3:13</td><td>Saturday: 1 Peter 4:8</td></tr>
<tr><td>Wednesday: James 1:19</td><td></td></tr>
</table>

Reflection

Conflict in marriage is inevitable, but how we handle it makes all the difference. The Bible provides practical wisdom on managing anger and preventing conflicts from escalating. Ephesians 4:26 reminds us not to let anger linger or allow conflicts to go unresolved. This is key to maintaining a healthy, peaceful marriage.

As a father and husband, it's important to approach conflicts with your wife in a way that seeks resolution and understanding rather than allowing disagreements to create distance. While every marriage experiences moments of tension, God's Word teaches us that resolving conflicts quickly and with love can protect the unity of our relationships.

In James 1:19, we are reminded to be quick to listen, slow to speak, and slow to become angry. This is a powerful guide for dealing with conflict in marriage. Listening carefully to your wife's concerns and responding with patience can prevent misunderstandings from turning into bigger issues.

One common mistake is letting small irritations build up over time. Addressing conflicts calmly and with grace helps avoid unnecessary strife. It's important to remember that marriage is a partnership, and conflicts should not be viewed as battles to win but as opportunities to grow together.

Forgiveness is also a crucial part of resolving conflict. Colossians 3:13 encourages us to forgive one another as Christ forgave us. Letting go of grudges and choosing forgiveness helps heal wounds and strengthens the bond between you and your wife.

Conflict resolution is a skill that requires humility, patience, and a willingness to prioritize the health of your marriage. By seeking peace and practicing forgiveness, you can overcome conflicts with your wife and create a stronger, more loving relationship.

Action Steps

1. **Pause Before Reacting**: The next time you feel frustration or anger rising during a conflict, take a moment to pause. Pray for wisdom and patience before responding. This small step can help diffuse the tension and create space for a calm discussion.

2. **Practice Active Listening**: During conflicts, focus on listening to your wife's perspective without interrupting. Repeat back what you hear to ensure understanding. This shows respect and can help uncover underlying issues that need to be addressed.

3. **Apologize and Forgive Quickly**: Make it a habit to apologize sincerely when you're in the wrong and to offer forgiveness when needed. Even if the conflict seems minor, apologizing can prevent further hurt and restore peace in your marriage.

By implementing these steps, you can approach conflicts in your marriage with a spirit of reconciliation and understanding. Avoiding prolonged disputes and practicing forgiveness helps create an atmosphere of love and respect in your home.

Closing Prayer

Dear Heavenly Father, Thank You for the gift of my wife and for the love we share. I ask for Your guidance in resolving any conflicts that arise in our marriage. Help me to approach every disagreement with patience, humility, and a desire for peace.

Lord, teach me to listen with an open heart and to respond with grace. When anger or frustration comes, remind me to turn to You for wisdom and strength. Help us to forgive one another quickly and to never let conflict come between us.

Please protect our marriage from division and strife. May Your love be the foundation of our relationship, and may we always seek to honor You in how we communicate with and care for each other. In Jesus' name, I pray. Amen.

Week 41: Building Emotional Resilience

"The joy of the Lord is your strength." (Nehemiah 8:10, NIV)

Daily Bible Reading

Sunday: Nehemiah 8:10
Monday: Philippians 4:13
Tuesday: Isaiah 40:31
Wednesday: Psalm 46:1-2

Thursday: 2 Corinthians 12:9
Friday: Psalm 23:4
Saturday: 1 Peter 5:7

Reflection

Parenting can often feel like an emotional marathon. From managing tantrums, disciplining with love, to navigating teenage mood swings, the emotional toll of fatherhood can be overwhelming. You're constantly giving, constantly present, and at times, you might feel like you're running on empty. The demands of being a dad, combined with the stresses of work and other responsibilities, can leave you feeling worn out emotionally and spiritually.

Nehemiah 8:10 reminds us that the joy of the Lord is our strength. This joy is not dependent on our circumstances or emotional state but is rooted in the unchanging presence and goodness of God. When you feel drained or emotionally stretched thin, God invites you to find your strength in Him, rather than in your own capacity to keep going.

Think of the moments when your patience runs low, or when you feel like you can't handle one more sibling argument or work deadline. In these moments, God calls you to rely on His strength. Emotional resilience comes not from suppressing or denying your emotions but from finding renewal in God's joy. His joy lifts you when you're overwhelmed and empowers you to keep showing up for your family.

Fathers often feel the pressure to hold it all together for their families, to be the steady rock that everyone can lean on. But the truth is, you don't have to carry the emotional load on your own. God is your refuge and strength, an ever-present help in times of trouble (Psalm 46:1). When you admit your weariness and turn to Him, you'll discover a deeper reservoir of emotional resilience.

In parenting, resilience looks like enduring the tough days with grace, learning to rest in God's presence when you feel emotionally exhausted, and trusting that His strength is enough. As you draw on the joy of the Lord, you'll be able to persevere, even when fatherhood feels overwhelming.

Action Steps

Here are a few practical steps to help you build emotional resilience this week:

1. **Daily Quiet Time with God**: Set aside 10-15 minutes each day for prayer and reflection. Use this time to hand over your emotional burdens to God, whether it's a rough day with the kids, stress from work, or personal struggles. Let His joy refresh and renew your heart during this quiet time. Start your day or end your day in His presence and allow His peace to center you.

2. **Create Space for Rest**: Emotional resilience is deeply tied to physical rest. Look at your schedule this week and carve out time to rest. Whether it's going for a walk, taking a short nap, or simply sitting in silence with a cup of coffee, allow yourself moments of pause to recharge. Remember that rest isn't a luxury; it's necessary for your emotional health.

3. **Reach Out for Support**: Don't carry emotional burdens alone. Whether it's your spouse, a trusted friend, or a fellow dad in your church, share your struggles with someone you trust. Talking about your emotional challenges can help release some of the pressure and remind you that you're not alone in this journey.

By implementing these steps, you'll find that emotional resilience comes not from pushing through on your own but from resting in God's strength and allowing space for renewal in your daily life.

Closing Prayer

Dear Heavenly Father,

Thank You for being my source of strength when I feel emotionally worn out. I acknowledge that there are times when the demands of parenting leave me drained, but I know that Your joy is my strength. Help me to draw from Your endless well of peace and renewal, and teach me to rest in Your presence when the pressures of life feel overwhelming.

Lord, guide me in setting aside time to recharge both emotionally and spiritually. Help me to remember that I don't have to carry every burden on my own. I surrender my struggles, my weariness, and my frustrations to You, trusting that You will lift me up.

Give me the grace to continue being present and loving toward my family, even on the hard days. Strengthen my heart and fill me with the joy that comes from knowing You are always with me. In Jesus' name, I pray. Amen.

Week 42: Teaching the Value of Hard Work

"Whatever you do, work at it with all your heart, as working for the Lord, not for human masters." (Colossians 3:23, NIV)

Daily Bible Reading

Sunday: Colossians 3:23

Monday: Proverbs 6:6-8

Tuesday: 2 Thessalonians 3:10

Wednesday: Ecclesiastes 9:10

Thursday: Proverbs 13:4

Friday: Galatians 6:9

Saturday: 1 Corinthians 15:58

Reflection

In today's fast-paced, convenience-driven culture, many children grow up with access to instant gratification—whether it's fast food, quick entertainment, or information at their fingertips. While modern conveniences have benefits, they also create a challenge for parents trying to instill the value of hard work in their children. How can we raise kids to understand the importance of diligence when everything around them seems so easy and effortless?

As fathers, we are called to model and teach the importance of hard work, not just for the sake of achieving success, but as an expression of service to God. Colossians 3:23 reminds us that whatever we do, we should work at it with all our heart as if working for the Lord. This perspective transforms labor from being just a task to an act of worship.

A strong work ethic helps build character, teaches responsibility, and gives children the tools to persevere through challenges. But more than that, it honors God. When we teach our children to work diligently, we are teaching them that their efforts matter, not just in the eyes of the world, but in the eyes of their Creator.

Consider the daily struggles of balancing your own work and family responsibilities. There are times when work feels like a grind, but remembering that your work is for God gives it purpose. The same applies to your children. Whether they are doing their homework, chores, or helping others, teaching them that their hard work is an offering to God shifts their perspective. It becomes less about duty and more about serving with love and excellence.

Real-life examples abound—think of the moments when your child faces a difficult task, perhaps in school or at home. Rather than rushing to make it easier for them, guide them through the process of working hard, even when it's uncomfortable. These lessons in perseverance, though hard in the moment, will stay with them for life. They will learn that effort and dedication are qualities that God values deeply.

Teaching this can be difficult, especially when we ourselves are often pulled toward shortcuts. However, modeling a strong work ethic in your own life and framing work as a God-honoring practice can plant seeds that grow into diligence and responsibility in your children.

Action Steps

Here are a few practical steps you can take this week to instill a strong work ethic in your children:

1. **Assign a Meaningful Responsibility**: This week, assign each of your children a task that requires effort and diligence, something that stretches them but is within their ability. It could be something like taking full responsibility for a household chore, preparing a simple meal, or completing a school project without help. Encourage them to approach it with their best effort, reminding them that they are working for the Lord.

2. **Discuss the Importance of Hard Work**: Have an intentional conversation with your children about the value of hard work. Use Colossians 3:23 to show them that their work, no matter how small, is important to God. Help them understand that hard work is not just about achieving results but about honoring God in the process. Emphasize that their efforts are seen by God and have eternal significance.

3. **Model Consistent Diligence**: Children learn best by example, so this week, make a point of showing your own commitment to hard work. Whether it's being diligent in your job, taking care of household tasks, or serving at church, let your children see that you approach your work with care and dedication. Share moments when work feels difficult but rewarding, and express how you are motivated to do your best because it honors God.

By implementing these steps, you'll begin to foster a culture of diligence and dedication in your home, one that values hard work not just for personal gain, but as a way to serve God and others.

Closing Prayer

Heavenly Father,

Thank You for the example You set in creating and sustaining all things. I come before You, asking for Your guidance as I teach my children the value of hard work. Help me to model diligence in a way that honors You, and give me the wisdom to guide my children as they grow in their responsibilities.

Lord, I pray that You would help my children see that their efforts, big or small, are valuable in Your eyes. Help them to work with joy, perseverance, and a heart that desires to please You above all else. When they face challenges, give them strength and patience to push through, knowing that You see and reward their efforts. In Jesus' name, I pray. Amen.

Week 43: Overcoming Fear in Fatherhood

"So do not fear, for I am with you; do not be dismayed, for I am your God. I will strengthen you and help you; I will uphold you with my righteous right hand." (Isaiah 41:10, NIV)

Daily Bible Reading

Sunday: Isaiah 41:10

Monday: Psalm 56:3-4

Tuesday: 2 Timothy 1:7

Wednesday: 1 Peter 5:7

Thursday: Philippians 4:6-7

Friday: Joshua 1:9

Saturday: Romans 8:15

Reflection

Fear is something that every father faces at some point in his journey. The fear of failing your children, not being able to provide, or being inadequate in leading your family spiritually can weigh heavily on your heart. These fears, if not dealt with, can lead to anxiety and frustration, and may even create distance between you and your family.

The reality is that being a father is an enormous responsibility. You are tasked with guiding your children, providing for them, protecting them, and being a spiritual leader in your home. With such weighty expectations, it's natural to fear making mistakes. But fear, when unchecked, can paralyze you. It can keep you from being the father God has called you to be.

Isaiah 41:10 offers a powerful reminder of God's presence. It tells us that we do not need to fear, not because we are perfect fathers, but because God is with us. He strengthens us, helps us, and upholds us. As fathers, we can take great comfort in knowing that we are not alone in this journey. God is our source of strength, wisdom, and guidance, even in moments when we feel completely inadequate.

Take a moment to reflect on some of the fears you carry as a father. Perhaps it's the fear of not being able to provide financially for your family, or the fear of not knowing how to raise your children in faith. Maybe you are afraid of repeating the mistakes of your own father. These are all real and valid fears, but they are not greater than God's promises.

God's Word tells us repeatedly not to fear because He is with us. As fathers, we must learn to trust God with our fears, surrendering them to Him so that we can lead with confidence. You may not have all the answers, and that's okay. What matters is that you rely on the One who does. Through prayer and a relationship with God, you can overcome the fears that try to hold you back from being the father you desire to be.

Action Steps

Here are a few practical steps you can take this week to overcome fear in your role as a father:

1. **Write Down Your Greatest Fear**: Take a moment to honestly reflect on the fear that weighs most heavily on your heart. Write it down, and bring it before God in prayer. Ask Him to give you peace and to help you trust Him in that area. Writing it down helps you acknowledge the fear and actively work toward releasing it.
2. **Meditate on God's Promises**: Throughout the week, spend time meditating on scriptures that remind you of God's presence and strength, such as Isaiah 41:10 and Philippians 4:6-7. Let His promises soak into your heart and mind, and use them as a defense against the fear that tries to creep in.

3. **Have an Honest Conversation**: If you're comfortable, share your fear with your spouse or a close friend. Sometimes, simply voicing your fear to someone you trust can bring relief and perspective. They may offer encouragement or share how they've faced similar fears.

By taking these steps, you'll begin to shift your focus away from your fear and onto God's ability to strengthen and guide you. Trust that God is with you in this journey, and let His presence give you the courage to lead your family with confidence.

Closing Prayer

Heavenly Father, Thank You for Your constant presence in my life. I come before You with the fears I carry as a father—the fear of failure, inadequacy, and not measuring up to the expectations placed on me. Lord, I confess these fears to You, knowing that You are my strength and my help.

I ask that You would remove the fear that tries to paralyze me, and replace it with confidence in You. Remind me daily that I am not alone in this journey, and that You are guiding me every step of the way. Help me to trust in Your promises and to rely on Your strength, especially in moments of doubt.

Lord, I pray that I would lead my family with wisdom, courage, and faith. Help me to surrender my fears to You and to walk forward knowing that You are with me, upholding me with Your righteous hand.

In Jesus' name, I pray. Amen.

Week 44: Encouraging Your Children's Unique Gifts

"There are different kinds of gifts, but the same Spirit distributes them. There are different kinds of service, but the same Lord. There are different kinds of working, but in all of them and in everyone it is the same God at work." (1 Corinthians 12:4-6, NIV)

Daily Bible Reading

Sunday: 1 Corinthians 12:4-6

Monday: Romans 12:6-8

Tuesday: Matthew 25:14-30

Wednesday: Proverbs 22:6

Thursday: James 1:17

Friday: Ephesians 2:10

Saturday: Colossians 3:23-24

Reflection

As fathers, one of the great challenges we face is figuring out how to nurture the individual gifts our children possess. It can be overwhelming to identify their unique talents, especially when every child is so different. Some might be naturally inclined toward academics, while others show early promise in music, sports, or creative arts. The diversity in their skills can make us question whether we are equipped to guide them effectively. You might worry, "Am I doing enough to help them flourish?" or "What if I push them in the wrong direction?"

In 1 Corinthians 12:4-6, Paul speaks about the variety of gifts distributed by the same Spirit. This scripture is a powerful reminder that each gift is unique but comes from God with a purpose. As fathers, we are not expected to be experts in everything, but we are called to recognize and encourage the talents God has placed in our children. God, who created each of our children with a plan, will also give us the wisdom and patience to guide them according to His will.

When a father feels unsure about how to nurture his child's gifts, it's important to step back and seek God's guidance. Consider the father of two sons: one who excels in science and another in sports. At times, it may seem impossible to support both equally, especially if the father feels out of his depth in either area. But just as God equips us for fatherhood, He will also equip us to guide our children toward using their talents for His glory.

Encouraging your children's gifts doesn't mean having all the answers. It means being there to support, guide, and remind them that their talents are a blessing from God. The goal is not to perfect their abilities but to help them discover how their gifts can serve others and honor God. When you view your role through this lens, you shift from trying to shape their talents into something specific to fostering their potential as God intended.

Our job as fathers is to recognize the talents our children have and encourage them to pursue these gifts with joy and purpose. The journey is not just about achieving success but about understanding that God has given these gifts for a reason. Trust that God will help you nurture your child's talents in a way that honors His plan.

Action Steps

Here are some practical steps to encourage and nurture your child's unique gifts this week:

1. **Have a Conversation About Their Talents**: Set aside time to talk to your child about what they enjoy and where they think their strengths lie. This conversation can help you understand their interests more deeply and give them a chance to express what excites them. Ask open-ended questions like, "What do you enjoy most about doing this?" or "How do you feel when you use this skill?"
2. **Create Opportunities for Exploration**: Help your child find ways to develop their talents by offering opportunities to

explore them further. If they love art, provide materials and time for them to create. If they're interested in music, consider lessons or exposing them to different instruments. The key is not to pressure them into excelling but to give them the space and tools to develop their skills in a way that feels natural and enjoyable.

3. **Pray for Wisdom**: Ask God to guide you in supporting your child's talents. Pray specifically for the ability to see their gifts clearly and to help them use these talents for His glory. This week, make it a habit to pray over your child's strengths, asking for God's direction in how to encourage them and foster growth in their unique abilities.

By creating an open, supportive environment, you allow your child to explore their talents with confidence, knowing they have both your encouragement and God's guidance.

Closing Prayer

Dear Heavenly Father, Thank You for the wonderful gifts You have placed in my children. I am grateful for the unique talents and abilities that You have entrusted to them. Please help me as a father to nurture and encourage these gifts in a way that honors You. Give me the wisdom to guide them, the patience to support them, and the discernment to recognize where You are leading them.

Lord, help my children to see that their talents are not just for their own gain but for Your glory. May they grow in confidence as they explore their gifts and find ways to use them to serve others. Grant me the grace to be a source of encouragement and love, even when I feel unsure or overwhelmed. I trust in Your perfect plan for their lives and ask for Your guidance every step of the way. In Jesus' name, I pray. Amen.

Week 45: Leading Through Conflict

"A gentle answer turns away wrath, but a harsh word stirs up anger." (Proverbs 15:1, NIV)

Daily Bible Reading

Sunday: Proverbs 15:1

Monday: Ephesians 4:26-27

Tuesday: Matthew 18:15

Wednesday: Colossians 3:13

Thursday: James 1:19-20

Friday: Romans 12:18

Saturday: 1 Peter 3:8

Reflection

Conflict is a reality in every family. Whether it's between you and your spouse or among your children, disagreements can quickly escalate, leading to hurt feelings and unresolved issues. As a father, your role is not just to resolve these conflicts, but to lead through them with wisdom and grace. This can feel overwhelming, especially when emotions run high and it seems easier to react impulsively. However, Proverbs 15:1 reminds us that a gentle answer can defuse anger, while harsh words will only escalate the situation.

The responsibility of being a father includes setting an example for how to handle conflict in a God-honoring way. This requires a calm heart, prayerful wisdom, and the ability to listen before speaking. When faced with a disagreement in your family, the natural reaction may be frustration or defensiveness. However, in those moments, your family is looking to you for leadership. How you respond to tension will often dictate how your family follows suit.

Let's imagine a situation where your children are arguing over a shared toy, and tempers are flaring. As a father, your initial reaction might be to raise your voice and demand peace. But stepping back, taking a breath, and responding with a gentle and firm tone can shift the dynamic. This doesn't mean avoiding discipline or correction, but approaching the conflict in a way that mirrors God's love and patience with us.

Jesus Himself demonstrated how to lead through conflict by staying calm and focusing on reconciliation. In Matthew 18:15, Jesus outlines a process for resolving disagreements by addressing the issue with grace and seeking peace. As fathers, we can apply this model in our homes, encouraging open communication and understanding, while addressing the root of the conflict rather than letting it fester.

Family conflict can either become an opportunity for growth or a breeding ground for resentment. When you lead with prayerful wisdom and a gentle spirit, you not only help resolve the issue at hand but also teach your children how to navigate future conflicts with grace. Trust God to give you the patience and discernment to lead your family well, even through challenging moments of disagreement.

Action Steps

Here are some practical steps you can take to lead your family through conflict this week:

1. **Pause and Pray**: Before reacting to any family disagreement, take a moment to pause and pray for wisdom. Ask God to give you the patience and the right words to diffuse the situation. This simple act can make a significant difference in how you respond, allowing you to approach the issue calmly rather than with frustration.
2. **Encourage Open Communication**: Create a space where family members can express their concerns or frustrations openly and respectfully. Teach your children how to articulate their feelings without attacking others, and model this

behavior yourself. When everyone feels heard, it's easier to move toward a resolution without anger taking control.

3. **Mediate with Wisdom**: When you find yourself in the middle of a family conflict, act as a mediator who seeks to understand both sides before offering solutions. Encourage everyone involved to listen to each other and work together to find a compromise. This approach fosters unity and teaches your children the value of resolving conflict in a peaceful manner.

By implementing these steps, you can create an environment where conflicts are addressed with wisdom and love rather than anger. This week, commit to leading through any disagreements in your home with a heart focused on reconciliation and peace, just as God leads us.

Closing Prayer

Dear Heavenly Father, Thank You for the wisdom found in Your Word. I ask for Your guidance as I lead my family through the conflicts and disagreements that arise in our home. Help me to respond with gentleness and patience, even when tensions are high. Give me the discernment to mediate with wisdom and to encourage peaceful resolutions that honor You.

Lord, I pray that You would teach me and my family how to navigate conflict in a way that reflects Your love and grace. Let us be quick to listen, slow to speak, and slow to anger. May we seek peace and unity in every situation, trusting in Your presence to guide us. Please give me the strength to lead by example, modeling the same forgiveness and understanding that You show to us. In Jesus' name, I pray. Amen.

Week 46: Setting Healthy Boundaries

"Above all else, guard your heart, for everything you do flows from it." (Proverbs 4:23, NIV)

Daily Bible Reading

Sunday: Proverbs 4:23

Monday: Ephesians 5:15-16

Tuesday: Colossians 3:23

Wednesday: Matthew 6:33

Thursday: 1 Corinthians 6:12

Friday: Psalm 90:12

Saturday: Galatians 5:1

Reflection

As a father, it can feel nearly impossible to balance the demands of work, family, and personal time. The pressure to provide, nurture, and lead can easily cause you to lose sight of healthy boundaries. When work spills into family time or you find yourself constantly distracted by other commitments, it's your loved ones and your spiritual well-being that pay the price.

Proverbs 4:23 emphasizes the importance of guarding your heart. This doesn't just apply to resisting sinful influences; it also means protecting your time and energy so you can serve your family effectively. A lack of boundaries drains you emotionally and spiritually, making it harder to engage with your children or your spouse. The problem arises when we confuse busyness with productivity, or when we fail to say "no" to things that steal our time and peace.

Consider a father who, after a long day of work, feels too tired to play with his children or spend time with his spouse. His mind is still focused on the tasks of the day, even though he is physically at home. He might tell himself that he's doing it all for his family, but without clear boundaries, his presence is diminished. His family misses the emotional connection he once provided.

Setting healthy boundaries allows you to be more present and effective as a father. This isn't about shutting down your responsibilities but making sure your family and faith come first. Boundaries enable you to create space for rest, for prayer, and for meaningful family time.

It's also important to model boundaries for your children. They observe how you prioritize and protect time, learning that it's okay to set limits on distractions, even if it's difficult. When your children see you prioritizing time with them, it teaches them to value relationships and faith over constant busyness.

The challenge for fathers is often guilt—thinking that setting boundaries is selfish or weak. But in reality, boundaries are a way of honoring God and your family. When you say "no" to the things that drain you, you say "yes" to deeper, more meaningful connections with those you love.

Action Steps

Here are practical steps to begin setting healthy boundaries in your life this week:

1. **Identify One Area Needing Boundaries**: Take some time to reflect on where your boundaries are weakest. It could be answering work emails during family time, or maybe it's allowing distractions to interfere with your personal time with God. Write down one area where you know you need better boundaries and be specific about how it impacts your family or spiritual life.

2. **Create a Plan to Protect That Space**: After identifying an area, create a simple plan to protect it. If it's work intruding on family time, set a firm cut-off time for work each day. If it's distractions during your prayer or Bible time, set aside a specific, uninterrupted block of time each morning or evening

to connect with God. Stick to your plan and let your family know your intentions so they can support you.

3. **Be Intentional About Guarding Your Heart**: Boundaries start with your heart. Each day, take a moment to reflect on what's most important to you—your relationship with God, your family, and your spiritual health. When you guard your heart by keeping these priorities in place, you can make better decisions about how to spend your time and energy.

Implementing these steps will help you not only restore balance but also protect the most important relationships in your life. This week, make the effort to set and enforce these boundaries, trusting that it will strengthen your role as a father and leader in your home.

Closing Prayer

Dear Heavenly Father, Thank You for reminding me of the importance of setting healthy boundaries. Help me to guard my heart and prioritize the things that matter most—my relationship with You and my family. Give me the wisdom to recognize where I need better boundaries and the strength to enforce them, even when it's difficult.

Lord, I surrender the pressures that pull me away from my family and my faith. Help me to let go of the distractions that drain my time and energy, so I can be fully present with my loved ones. Guide me in leading my family with love and intention, showing them how to balance life with Your wisdom.

I pray that You give me the patience and grace to stay committed to these boundaries, knowing that they will bring greater peace and purpose to my home. Thank You for being my source of strength and wisdom in all things.

In Jesus' name, I pray. Amen.

Week 47: Building Strong Friendships as a Christian Father

"A friend loves at all times, and a brother is born for a time of adversity." (Proverbs 17:17, NIV)

Daily Bible Reading

Sunday: Proverbs 17:17

Monday: John 15:13

Tuesday: Ecclesiastes 4:9-10

Wednesday: 1 Thessalonians 5:11

Thursday: Proverbs 27:17

Friday: Philippians 2:4

Saturday: Colossians 3:12-13

Reflection

Friendships play a crucial role in every man's life, yet as fathers, we often find ourselves struggling to maintain close relationships due to the demands of family, work, and other responsibilities. Proverbs 17:17 reminds us of the value of friendships: true friends love consistently and support us through difficult times. As fathers, cultivating strong, meaningful friendships is not just important for our own well-being, but it also sets an example for our children about the value of loyalty, support, and community.

However, the balance between being a dedicated father and husband while nurturing friendships can be tricky. Many fathers feel guilty about spending time with friends, worrying it might take away from their family. Yet, friendships are a source of encouragement, accountability, and wisdom, which can make us better husbands and fathers. Ecclesiastes 4:9-10 illustrates the strength found in companionship: two are better than one because they can help each other succeed and lift each other up in times of need.

In John 15:13, Jesus exemplifies the ultimate friendship by laying down His life for His friends. While we may not need to sacrifice our lives, this verse highlights the importance of sacrificial love and commitment in our friendships. Strong friendships require effort, patience, and sometimes sacrifice, but the rewards are immeasurable.

As fathers, our friendships also serve as a support network that helps us grow spiritually and emotionally. Proverbs 27:17 reminds us that just as iron sharpens iron, one man sharpens another. Surrounding ourselves with godly friends strengthens our faith and provides the accountability needed to navigate the challenges of fatherhood.

It's important to teach our children the value of friendship by modeling it in our own lives. When they see us investing in healthy, supportive friendships, they learn how to form and maintain relationships that reflect Christ's love.

Action Steps

1. **Prioritize One Friendship**: Identify one friend you may have unintentionally neglected due to the busyness of life. Reach out to them this week, even if it's just a phone call or message, and commit to maintaining that relationship moving forward.
2. **Schedule Time for Fellowship**: Set aside intentional time, even if it's once a month, to meet with friends for coffee, prayer, or conversation. Building strong friendships requires intentionality, and scheduling time with your friends will help ensure that these relationships are nurtured.
3. **Teach Your Children About Friendship**: Have a conversation with your children about the importance of friendships. Share stories from your own life about times when friends have been there for you, and encourage them to cultivate relationships with others who reflect godly values.

By taking these steps, you can build and strengthen friendships that uplift and encourage you as a father while also demonstrating the value of true friendship to your children.

Closing Prayer

Heavenly Father, Thank You for the gift of friendship and for the people You've placed in my life who support and encourage me. Help me to be a faithful friend who reflects Your love to others. Guide me as I seek to balance my responsibilities as a father while also nurturing the friendships You've blessed me with.

Lord, teach me to be intentional in maintaining these relationships and to invest in the lives of others, just as they invest in mine. Help me to model godly friendship for my children, so they can grow to value the blessings of true community.

In moments of weariness or stress, remind me to lean on my friends for support and to offer them the same in return. Strengthen the bonds of friendship in my life and help me to be the friend that others need.

In Jesus' name, I pray. Amen.

Week 48: Recognizing and Avoiding Bad Friendships That Can Harm Your Marriage

"Do not be misled: 'Bad company corrupts good character.'"
(1 Corinthians 15:33, NIV)

Daily Bible Reading

Sunday: 1 Corinthians 15:33

Monday: Proverbs 13:20

Tuesday: Proverbs 27:6

Wednesday: James 4:4

Thursday: 1 Peter 2:11

Friday: Matthew 5:29-30

Saturday: Psalm 1:1-2

Reflection

Friendships are an essential part of life, providing support, encouragement, and accountability. However, not all friendships are beneficial—some can subtly erode the foundation of your marriage. 1 Corinthians 15:33 warns us that "bad company corrupts good character." As Christian fathers and husbands, it's vital to recognize when certain friendships may be pulling us away from our family or influencing us in ways that negatively impact our marriage.

Bad friendships can take many forms. Sometimes they might involve individuals who encourage unhealthy behaviors, like neglecting family responsibilities or speaking poorly about your spouse. Proverbs 13:20 teaches us to "walk with the wise and become wise, for a companion of fools suffers harm." Friends who don't respect the sanctity of marriage or who lead us down a path of selfishness or temptation can weaken the bonds we have with our spouse.

One of the dangers is that these influences may not always be obvious at first. Proverbs 27:6 says, "Wounds from a friend can be trusted, but an enemy multiplies kisses." True friends will tell us hard truths, even if it's uncomfortable, whereas a bad friend might flatter and lead us astray with empty encouragement or unhealthy advice. Recognizing these subtle red flags in our friendships is crucial to protecting our marriage.

In James 4:4, the Bible warns about being too close to the world's values, and this can apply to friendships that promote materialism, unfaithfulness, or disregard for family priorities. It's important to align our friendships with those who uphold the values we strive to live by.

As husbands and fathers, we need to set healthy boundaries to ensure that our friendships strengthen, rather than weaken, our marriages. If a friendship is causing tension between you and your spouse, it's time to reassess its influence. Psalm 1:1 reminds us of the blessing that comes from not walking in the counsel of the wicked but delighting in the law of the Lord.

Action Steps

1. **Evaluate Your Friendships**: Take some time to reflect on the influence your friends have on your marriage. Ask yourself: Do they encourage you to be a better husband and father? Do they respect your marriage and the commitment you've made to your spouse? If certain friendships are leading you in the wrong direction, it may be time to create distance.
2. **Set Boundaries**: For friends who have a negative impact, establish clear boundaries. This might mean limiting the time spent with them or avoiding certain conversations that could harm your marriage. Be firm but kind in explaining the importance of prioritizing your family over unhealthy influences.

3. **Seek Godly Friendships**: Actively seek out friends who share your faith and values, especially those who encourage you in your role as a husband and father. Proverbs 27:17 says, "As iron sharpens iron, so one person sharpens another." Surround yourself with people who help strengthen your marriage and spiritual life.

By recognizing and addressing toxic friendships, you can protect your marriage and focus on building relationships that align with your values and commitments. Your marriage will grow stronger when you prioritize healthy influences and set boundaries where necessary.

Closing Prayer

Heavenly Father, Thank You for the friendships You have placed in my life. I ask for Your wisdom and guidance to discern between friends who lift me up and those who may lead me astray. Help me to recognize any relationships that negatively influence my marriage or pull me away from my commitment as a husband and father.

Lord, grant me the courage to set healthy boundaries where needed, and give me the strength to walk away from friendships that are harmful to my family. Surround me with godly friends who encourage and support me in living a life that honors You and strengthens my marriage.

Help me to be a good friend in return, always speaking truth in love and encouraging others to walk faithfully in their relationships. Protect my marriage, and let it be a reflection of Your love and grace.

In Jesus' name, I pray. Amen.

Week 49: Teaching Contentment in a Material World

"I know what it is to be in need, and I know what it is to have plenty. I have learned the secret of being content in any and every situation, whether well fed or hungry, whether living in plenty or in want. I can do all this through him who gives me strength."

(Philippians 4:12-13, NIV)

Daily Bible Reading

Sunday: Philippians 4:12-13

Monday: 1 Timothy 6:6-8

Tuesday: Luke 12:15

Wednesday: Hebrews 13:5

Thursday: Matthew 6:19-21

Friday: Proverbs 30:8-9

Saturday: Psalm 37:16

Reflection

In today's world, we are bombarded with the idea that more possessions equal more happiness. Advertisements, social media, and even peers promote a lifestyle where material gain is prioritized. As Christian fathers, one of our most challenging tasks is teaching our children to find contentment, not in what they own, but in their relationship with Christ.

Philippians 4:12-13 gives us a beautiful reminder from the apostle Paul: true contentment is not about how much or how little we have. Paul, who experienced both wealth and poverty, learned that his joy and satisfaction were rooted in his relationship with Jesus, not his circumstances. This is a lesson we must pass on to our children, especially in a society that places immense value on material wealth.

It's easy for children to get caught up in the comparison game. Whether it's comparing toys, clothes, or gadgets with their friends, the desire to "keep up" can be strong. As fathers, we must guide them to understand that lasting fulfillment comes from something much deeper. Proverbs 30:8-9 reflects a prayer for balance: asking neither for poverty nor riches, but simply enough to meet daily needs. This attitude of reliance on God's provision teaches humility and gratitude.

One way to help our children grasp contentment is to model it ourselves. If we're constantly chasing after the latest trends or complaining about what we lack, our children will pick up on those attitudes. But when we show gratitude for what we already have and trust God to meet our needs, they will see the peace that comes from contentment in Christ.

At the heart of this lesson is helping our children understand that their value isn't tied to their belongings. Just as Jesus warned in Luke 12:15, "Life does not consist in an abundance of possessions," we need to teach our children to value their relationship with God and others over what they own. This may require difficult conversations and intentional efforts, but it's essential in helping them navigate the materialism of today's world.

Action Step

1. **Practice Gratitude as a Family**: This week, take time as a family to practice gratitude. Each day, ask your children to list one thing they are thankful for that isn't material. This could be family, friends, their health, or an experience they enjoyed. Encourage them to recognize blessings that go beyond what they own. Writing these down in a family gratitude journal can help create a habit of focusing on non-material blessings.

2. **Limit Material Comparisons**: Discuss with your children the dangers of comparing themselves to others based on possessions. Remind them of the scripture, "Life does not consist in an abundance of possessions" (Luke 12:15). Use real-

life examples or even share personal stories from your own experience to show how comparison can steal joy. Help them to celebrate the blessings they have and be content with what God has provided.

3. **Set a Family Goal of Giving**: To further instill the value of contentment, set a goal to give as a family. Whether it's donating clothes, toys, or time to those in need, this action teaches that happiness doesn't come from acquiring more but from giving to others. Let your children help in the decision-making process, and explain that contentment is also about knowing we have enough to give back.

By focusing on these practical steps, you can create a culture of contentment in your home and teach your children that real fulfillment comes from their relationship with God, not the material things they own.

Closing Prayer

Heavenly Father, Thank You for being our ultimate provider. We acknowledge that everything we have comes from You, and we trust in Your goodness to meet our needs. Help us to find contentment, not in material possessions, but in Your presence and provision.

Lord, teach us as fathers to model a life of gratitude and contentment before our children. Guide us in helping them understand that true happiness is found in You, not in the things of this world. May we not be swayed by the materialistic values around us, but instead focus on storing up treasures in heaven.

Help us to be grateful for the blessings You've given us, and give us the wisdom to teach our children to do the same. Lead us to be generous with what we have, and help us find joy in giving rather than receiving. In Jesus' name, we pray. Amen.

Week 50: Preparing for Changes in Fatherhood

"There is a time for everything, and a season for every activity under the heavens." (Ecclesiastes 3:1, NIV)

Daily Bible Reading

Sunday: Ecclesiastes 3:1

Monday: 1 Corinthians 13:11

Tuesday: Psalm 127:3-5

Wednesday: Isaiah 43:18-19

Thursday: James 1:5

Friday: Proverbs 22:6

Saturday: Malachi 4:6

Reflection

Fatherhood is a role marked by constant change. From the moment a child is born, the father's responsibilities shift and grow with each passing year. As children develop, fathers experience a range of transitions—from sleepless nights with a newborn to the bittersweet milestones of sending a child off to school or beyond. These changes can be exciting, but they can also bring anxiety, uncertainty, and the realization that we cannot always control the outcomes we desire.

Ecclesiastes 3:1 reminds us that everything in life happens in seasons. Just as the natural world cycles through seasons of growth and rest, fatherhood comes with its own phases. The key is embracing each season with grace and flexibility. Trying to hold onto the past or resist change only leads to frustration and disappointment. Instead, trusting that God's timing is perfect can help fathers navigate these transitions with peace.

One of the emotional challenges fathers often face is the feeling of being left behind as children become more independent. Whether it's dealing with a child becoming a teenager or handling the complexities of an adult child leaving home, fathers may wrestle with the shift in their role. This can bring a mix of pride, grief, and sometimes a sense of loss. Fathers may wonder, "Am I still needed?" But God calls us to lean into these transitions and recognize that while our role changes, it is no less important. We must trust that God is still at work in our children's lives even as they grow and develop into individuals with their own paths.

Practical challenges also arise when the dynamics of family life shift. It's common to feel like you're being pulled in different directions, particularly when children need different kinds of support at various stages. The season when children are young and require constant care looks very different from the season when they are teenagers, needing more guidance but seeking independence. Each phase requires us to adapt and shift our approach to parenting.

A powerful way to embrace these seasons is to ask for God's wisdom, as James 1:5 encourages. Changes may bring anxiety or fear, but when we seek God's counsel, He can provide the clarity and peace we need to navigate them. By acknowledging the inevitability of change and seeking God's guidance, we can learn to embrace the new phases of fatherhood with confidence.

Action Step

1. **Reflect on an Upcoming Change**: Take time to reflect on a significant change happening in your family life. Perhaps your child is transitioning from one school level to another, becoming more independent, or leaving home for the first time. Instead of focusing on what you may lose, reflect on the ways God might be working in your child's life and in your role as a father. Ask God to show you how you can best support your child through this transition, while also adjusting your own mindset about your evolving role.

2. **Pray for Wisdom and Peace**: Change often brings uncertainty and fear of the unknown. Spend time in prayer, asking God to grant you wisdom as you navigate this new season of fatherhood. Trust in His promise in James 1:5 to generously give wisdom to those who ask. Hand over your worries, knowing that He will provide the clarity and strength you need to be the father your child requires in this phase.

3. **Be Present in the Current Season**: One of the best ways to prepare for change is to be fully engaged in the present moment. Take time to connect with your child at this stage of life, whether they are young or transitioning into adulthood. Be intentional in your conversations and create memories that reflect the love and support you have for them. This will not only strengthen your bond but also ease the transitions that come as they grow.

By reflecting, praying, and being fully present, you can navigate these transitions with grace and create a foundation of trust and love that will carry you and your children through all the seasons of fatherhood.

Closing Prayer

Heavenly Father, Thank You for the gift of fatherhood and for the many seasons of life You have given us to experience with our children. As we face changes in our families, help us to embrace these transitions with grace and trust in Your perfect timing. When we feel anxious or uncertain about what lies ahead, remind us that You are always with us, guiding and providing the wisdom we need.

Lord, grant us the strength to be present in each moment, and to love and support our children as they grow. In Jesus' name, we pray. Amen.

Week 51: Facing Financial Struggles

"And my God will meet all your needs according to the riches of his glory in Christ Jesus." (Philippians 4:19, NIV)

Daily Bible Reading

Sunday: Philippians 4:19

Monday: Matthew 6:31-33

Tuesday: Proverbs 3:9-10

Wednesday: 2 Corinthians 9:8

Thursday: Psalm 37:25

Friday: 1 Timothy 6:17

Saturday: Matthew 7:7-8

Reflection

Financial struggles are one of the most common and challenging burdens fathers face. The responsibility of providing for your family can feel overwhelming, especially when unexpected expenses arise or income isn't stretching far enough. You might ask yourself, "How can I give my family the life they deserve?" or "What if I can't meet their needs?"

These questions can create anxiety and stress, but Philippians 4:19 offers a comforting promise: "And my God will meet all your needs according to the riches of his glory in Christ Jesus." This verse reminds us that, while we are responsible for working and providing for our families, it is ultimately God who supplies all of our needs. He sees the pressures you face, and He knows the financial challenges that weigh on your heart.

It's important to remember that God's provision isn't always immediate or in the way we expect, but it is always sufficient. When facing financial difficulties, it's easy to feel like you're carrying the weight of the world on your shoulders. However, God invites you to trust in His abundance, not your own limited resources. He provides for us in ways we often overlook—through a sudden job opportunity, an unexpected financial gift, or even a shift in our perspective on what we truly need.

Consider the story of a father who loses his job unexpectedly. The immediate reaction might be fear—how will the bills be paid? How will the family make it through this season? In the midst of this uncertainty, the father prays for provision, and although no immediate solution comes, he begins to notice God providing in unexpected ways. Friends offer support, the family pulls together, and soon, a new job opportunity arises. Through this difficult season, the father learns that God's provision is not just about money—it's about trusting in His faithfulness even when the path isn't clear.

Another common struggle is the fear that you're not giving your children enough. The world constantly pressures fathers to measure their success by their financial status. It's easy to feel inadequate when you can't provide the latest gadgets or experiences for your children. But remember, God calls us to provide for our families in ways that go beyond material things. Time, love, and spiritual guidance are just as important as financial security. When you trust God with your finances, you can release the pressure of "keeping up" and instead focus on meeting the true needs of your family.

The practical realities of managing money can still feel daunting, and it's important to be wise with your resources. Creating a budget, managing expenses, and making sacrifices are all part of the responsibility of providing. But as you take these practical steps, do so with the peace of knowing that God is your ultimate provider. He has promised to meet all of your needs, and He will remain faithful.

The reality is that financial struggles will come and go, but God's provision is constant. When you shift your focus from fear to trust, you open the door for God to provide in ways you never imagined. And in doing so, you set an example for your children—showing them that true security comes not from wealth, but from reliance on God.

Action Step

This week, take practical steps to surrender your financial worries to God. Here are some actions you can take:

1. **Reflect on a Financial Blessing**: Take a moment to reflect on one financial blessing you've received recently. It could be something small, like a bill that was less than expected, or something larger, like a bonus at work. Write it down and thank God for His provision in that moment. This practice will help you recognize how God is meeting your needs, even in difficult times.
2. **Create a Family Prayer Time**: Sit down with your family and have an honest discussion about your finances. Encourage open communication about any worries or needs, and then pray together as a family. This will not only help you release your anxieties to God but will also teach your children the importance of trusting Him with their future.
3. **Budget with God's Help**: If financial management is a struggle, take time this week to create or revise your budget. But before you do, pray for wisdom. Ask God to guide you in making wise decisions about spending, saving, and giving. Include your family in this process so that they can learn the importance of financial stewardship and trust in God's provision.

By taking these steps, you'll be actively placing your trust in God's promise to provide for your family's needs. You'll also create an environment of transparency and trust in your household, where financial struggles can be discussed and prayed over together.

Closing Prayer

Heavenly Father, I come before You with the financial burdens that weigh on my heart. I want to provide for my family and give them everything they need, but sometimes the pressure feels overwhelming. Lord, I trust in Your promise in Philippians 4:19 — that You will meet all of our needs according to the riches of Your glory. Help me to release my anxieties to You, knowing that You are our ultimate provider. Guide me in managing our finances with wisdom and grace, and help me to be a good steward of the resources You've entrusted to me. Lord, I ask for peace in times of uncertainty and provision in times of need. Teach me to trust You fully, and let my family see Your hand at work in our lives. Thank You for Your faithfulness and for always meeting our needs. In Jesus' name, Amen.

Week 52: Finishing Strong as a Father

"Therefore, if anyone is in Christ, the new creation has come: The old has gone, the new is here!" (2 Corinthians 5:17, NIV)

Reflection

As we approach the end of the year, it's natural to reflect on the journey as a father—the triumphs, the challenges, and the mistakes. Sometimes, the mistakes we make can weigh heavily on our hearts, leaving us discouraged or questioning our effectiveness as fathers. We may remember times when we lost our patience, missed important moments, or struggled to balance family and work. These moments can lead us to feel like we've fallen short in our role as the spiritual leader and protector of our homes.

However, 2 Corinthians 5:17 reminds us of a powerful truth: in Christ, we are new creations. The mistakes of the past do not define us. Each day is an opportunity to live in the grace and renewal that Christ offers. The old has gone, and the new has come! This is not only true of our spiritual lives but also in how we approach fatherhood. Every day is a chance to learn from the past and grow into the father God calls us to be.

It's easy to focus on the mistakes and feel discouraged, but God's mercies are new every morning (Lamentations 3:22-23). He gives us fresh starts, no matter how we may have stumbled. The key is not to dwell on the past but to press forward, trusting that God is shaping us into better fathers through His grace.

Being a father is a journey, not a destination. Each year brings new lessons, growth, and challenges. As fathers, we need to give ourselves grace, just as God gives us grace. The enemy loves to remind us of our failures, but God reminds us of our potential. He sees the man He created, a father capable of leading his family with love, wisdom, and humility. If we can trust Him with our future, He will equip us with everything we need to finish strong.

As this year closes, remember that God isn't asking for perfection, but for faithfulness. Lean into His strength and know that every day is a new chance to be the father He designed you to be.

Action Steps

1. **Reflect on the Year with Gratitude and Grace**: Take time to look back on the past year, but instead of focusing on where you fell short, focus on God's faithfulness. Consider writing down the areas where you've grown as a father, thanking God for the ways He has guided and sustained you. Acknowledge the mistakes, but offer them up to God in prayer, knowing that His grace is sufficient to cover them.

2. **Set Goals for the Coming** Year: As you reflect on the past year, think about specific areas where you'd like to grow as a father in the coming year. These goals don't have to be grand gestures; they can be simple commitments like being more present at family meals, prioritizing your spiritual leadership at home, or spending more one-on-one time with your children. Write these goals down and commit them to God, asking for His help to accomplish them.

3. **Renew Your Daily Time with God**: Start the new year by renewing your personal time with God. Make prayer and

Bible study a priority in your daily routine. By staying grounded in God's Word and consistently seeking His wisdom, you'll be better equipped to handle the challenges of fatherhood with grace and strength. Even five minutes of quiet reflection and prayer can make a significant difference in your spiritual and emotional resilience.

By reflecting on the past, setting goals for the future, and renewing your relationship with God, you can finish the year strong and step into the new year with confidence and hope. Remember that God's grace is enough to cover all your shortcomings, and His strength will guide you in the journey ahead.

Closing Prayer

Heavenly Father, As this year comes to a close, I come before You with a heart full of gratitude and humility. I thank You for Your constant guidance, even when I have stumbled. You have walked with me through the challenges of fatherhood, and I trust that You will continue to lead me in the days to come.

I ask for Your forgiveness for the mistakes I've made and for the times I've fallen short as a father. Help me to release the burden of regret and to embrace the new opportunities You give me every day. Renew my spirit, and give me the strength to finish this year strong, knowing that in You, I am a new creation.

As I look ahead to the new year, I ask for Your wisdom and grace to lead my family with love, patience, and faithfulness. Guide me in my role as a father, and help me to grow in Your likeness each day. In Jesus' name, I pray. Amen.

Conclusion

As we bring this 52-week journey to a close, I hope that this devotional has been a source of encouragement, strength, and guidance for you as a father. The challenges of fatherhood are real, and navigating them requires not only wisdom and patience but also an unwavering dependence on God. Each week has addressed a different struggle, offering biblical insights and practical steps to help you grow both as a man and as a father.

Fatherhood is a lifelong calling. As much as we strive to raise our children with love, integrity, and faith, we must also remember that we are constantly growing ourselves. We will face moments of doubt, failure, and fear, but we must always lean into the grace and strength of our Heavenly Father. Just as we teach our children to rely on God, we must model that same trust and reliance on Him in our own lives.

Throughout this year, we've explored themes ranging from overcoming personal failures to fostering spiritual growth in our families. Along the way, we've been reminded of one foundational truth: that in all of our efforts, God is with us. His love for us as His children empowers us to love and lead our own children with compassion, humility, and faithfulness.

As you continue on your journey as a father, remember that every day is a new opportunity. It's not about achieving perfection, but about walking in faith, trusting in God's grace, and remaining committed to your family. The lessons learned this year are not confined to these pages but can serve as ongoing reminders of the high calling you have as a father.

My prayer for you is that you will continue to grow in your role as a father, trusting God in every season and circumstance. May

He give you the wisdom to guide your children, the strength to overcome the challenges, and the grace to love deeply, forgive freely, and lead with a heart that reflects His own.

As you step forward into the next phase of your journey, be confident that God has equipped you for every good work. You are not alone; He is with you every step of the way, empowering you to finish strong as the father He has called you to be.

Thank you for allowing me to walk alongside you through this devotional. May God continue to bless you and your family richly as you seek to honor Him in all that you do.

In Christ's love,

Tiffany Barker